RESPONDING TO ADULT LEARNERS IN HIGHER EDUCATION

D0146860

The Professional Practices in Adult Education and Human Resource Development Series explores issues and concerns of practitioners who work in the broad range of settings in adult and continuing education and human resource development.

The books are intended to provide information and strategies on how to make practice more effective for professionals and those they serve. They are written from a practical viewpoint and provide a forum for instructors, administrators, policy makers, counselors, trainers, managers, program and organizational developers, instructional designers, and other related professionals.

Michael W. Galbraith
Editor-in-Chief

RESPONDING TO ADULT LEARNERS IN HIGHER EDUCATION

Carol E. Kasworm
Cheryl J. Polson
Sarah Jane Fishback

KRIEGER PUBLISHING COMPANY
MALABAR, FLORIDA
2002

Original Edition 2002

Printed and Published by
KRIEGER PUBLISHING COMPANY
KRIEGER DRIVE
MALABAR, FLORIDA 32950

Library of Congress Cataloging-in-Publication Data

Kasworm, Carol E.
    Responding to adult learners in higher education / Carol E. Kasworm,
Cheryl J. Polson, Sarah Jane Fishback.
        p.   cm. — (Professional practices in adult education and human
        resource development series)
    Includes bibliographical references and index.
    ISBN 1-57524-109-9 (alk. paper)
    1. Adult education. 2. Education, Higher. 3. Universities and colleges—
Administration. I. Polson, Cheryl Jean. II. Fishback, Sarah Jane.
III. Title. IV. Series.
LC5215 .K28 2002
374—dc21   2001050431

10   9   8   7   6   5   4   3   2

CONTENTS

PREFACE

The fast pace and complexity of modern society have made "lifelong learning" more than a catch phrase. In increasing numbers, adults are turning to colleges and universities to help them cope with change both within themselves and in their worlds. They are seeking many goals that include upgrading their skills, preparing for new careers, or learning new knowledge to cope with pressures created by a rapidly changing environment. Too often, institutions of higher education fail to meet the challenges posed by these adult learners. Because many campuses have a strong historic commitment to traditional-aged, full-time residential students, they are blind to the adult learner as a very different type of student and participant in higher education. Higher education will best serve adult students when its programs and services respond to the diverse needs and circumstances of these older, mature learners.

We created this book as an informative, resource handbook to assist practitioners who interact daily with adult learners or who desire to recruit and serve adult learners as new clientele. *Responding to Adult Learners in Higher Education* can also serve as a practical tool for campus administrators in formulating campus policies, designing adult-learner-friendly higher education environments, and developing staff and faculty who proactively serve adult students. This book will provide an important sharing of ideas between adult and continuing educators and student service workers as they collaboratively serve adult students. For academic advisors, we hope that this book can assist their understanding not only of the advising process, but of their important role in adult students' lives. Through this book, faculty members are encouraged to reflect on their importance to the adult learner's connectedness to the institution and to create classroom environments that facilitate the creation of learning communities, as well as promote effective adult learning. Both student services professionals and those who teach in graduate programs for preparing such professionals are encouraged to use the book as a resource for understanding how adult learner needs can be identified and considered in campus programming and services. Finally, we hope that readers who are currently adult learners will find a commonality with the experiences and concerns reflected in the book.

Responding to Adult Learners in Higher Education addresses not only the complexity of adult learner lives, but also their unique motivations and past educational experiences. It also speaks to the diversity of higher education institutions and the multiple institutional formats through which adult learners pursue their educational goals. It recognizes that adult learners bring extremely diverse values, motives, needs, and experiences to the campus. They participate in significantly varied ways through a combination of formats and delivery systems that include credit, certificate, and post-baccalaureate involvement. They pursue daytime, evening, and weekend offerings, as well as distance delivery, accelerated or fast-tracked offerings, specialized adult degree programs, contract learning, and competency credit alternatives. Given this diversity, no uniform prescription can be provided to help institutions effectively address the needs of adult learners. We believe, however, that by carefully examining your adult student characteristics and campus environment, as well as considering each chapter within this book in relation to your campus and adult population, you should be able to formulate a strategic initiative to effectively respond to adult learners at your institution.

This book reflects our lives of commitment to our individual work with adult learners as well as our research to better understand and describe the adult undergraduate student. Shaped by practitioners' struggles to improve institutional services and support to adult learners, this book reflects these efforts by individuals and by institutions seeking to be adult learner oriented. This book also reflects our desire to integrate literature from three fields: adult education, college student personnel, and the broader field of higher education. Bringing together the concepts and understandings of these three disciplines is critical to effectively serving adult learners. Examples of good practice are also woven throughout each chapter to serve the readership. These examples provide concrete illustrations of how institutions can adapt institutional practices and offerings that respond to the needs and circumstances of adult learners.

Responding to Adult Learners in Higher Education has seven chapters. The introductory chapter provides a broad overview of the current national statistics and related research findings on adult college student characteristics. To effectively respond to adult learners in higher education, individual institutions need to take steps to understand the characteristics of currently enrolled adult learners, their enrollment patterns, and their life circumstances. This chapter presents a number of strategies for gathering information about adult learners, including personal interviews, demographic surveys, and focus groups. Pivotal to this chapter is the recognition that adults as a group of students are more mature, have complex life experiences, and are significantly more heterogeneous than those who are younger.

In Chapters 2 and 3, we concentrate on the critical issues of recruiting and retaining adult students from both the adult learner and the institutional perspective. Chapter 2 considers the dynamics of the entry or reentry process and factors that influence student persistence. Barriers to enrollment and persistence are also addressed, followed by a discussion of characteristics that differentiate adult persisters and nonpersisters. Effective recruitment and retention programs require an understanding of adult motives and goals, influences on adult collegiate entry, and factors influencing subsequent enrollment. Chapter 3 identifies institutional strategies and policies that influence the admission and retention of adult students. We discuss marketing techniques, including Web-based marketing. Institutional strategies for increasing adult learner retention are also discussed. We stress that recruitment efforts should reflect the institution's vision of academic programs, delivery systems, and support services that are both oriented to adult learners and consistent with the institution's mission. Retention is based on adult-oriented environments that support adult life styles, support systems for learner entry and continuance, and linkages between the world of adults and the institution.

Academic advising is the subject of Chapter 4. We examine the various challenges adults encounter throughout their college attendance and how these challenges dictate that academic advising be a continuous process. A description of the academic advising process is provided, with specific questions to be explored at each stage. The chapter concludes with an advisor checklist. We stress that academic advising should offer a number of services—providing information, removing barriers, presenting options, facilitating decision making, and making connections with needed resources. Advising should help students set realistic goals, make connections between their life goals and their educational objectives, and become more effective in decision making by dealing knowledgeably and flexibly with transitions.

Chapter 5 addresses the importance of creating connecting classrooms and learning communities for adult learners. We explore the ultimate importance of the connecting classroom for adult lives. We also examine how adult student differences affect classroom involvement based on the students' beliefs about knowledge expertise and about the college's culture. Key aspects of the psychological, physical, social, and intellectual adult learning climates are discussed. Lastly, the varied types of learning communities are explored—from face-to-face classrooms through intentional clustering of adult courses, adult cohort degree programs, self-directed learning structures, and recent efforts to create learning community in cyberspace.

The need for student services targeted to adult learner concerns is discussed in Chapter 6. We examine orientation programs, academic and learning assistance, and the career or personal counseling needs of this student population. A discussion of the one-stop information center and its variations, designed specifically for adult learners, is included. We stress the need for an institution-wide approach to ensure that existing student services consider adult students' needs and include strategies for providing responsive programs. Communicating the availability of relevant student services to off-campus learners is discussed, as is the need to provide alternative resources to those unable to access campus-based resources.

The final chapter is devoted to strategies for ensuring effective advocacy for adult learners. The initial emphasis is on creating an institutional awareness. We suggest ways to determine how adult learners perceive the campus environment as well as the development of strategies for influencing institutional change. Assuring fair and equitable treatment from all aspects of the institution remains a critical goal. Adult learner advocates are pivotal to reaching this goal because they raise important questions, encourage others to examine critical issues, and facilitate changes needed to increase institution-wide responsiveness to adult learners.

The book concludes with appendixes that include a select listing of professional associations and a sample introductory workshop to create awareness of adult student learner characteristics and needs.

We hope this book offers to each of you informative and practical ways to increase the effectiveness of your work, as well as enhance the broader agenda of higher education in serving adult students. It is our hope that, as a reader of this book, you will gain a more complex understanding of adult learners, have a renewed and stimulated commitment to serving adult learners, and have identified additional strategies for making the higher education experience a more successful one for your adult learners.

ACKNOWLEDGMENTS

We wish to express our sincere appreciation to the many individuals who have shared their experiences, concerns, and suggestions in the development of this book. Our work has been a labor of love. We have been inspired by the many adult learners in our classrooms and by the many faculty and staff in institutions serving these individuals. We have also found significant insights through our research, our professional work, and our practitioner involvements in the joys, hopes, and dilemmas of fostering an adult-supportive collegiate environment. To the many practitioners who have envisioned and created better worlds for adult learners, we applaud you and recognize your creative innovations.

The evolution of this book was fostered through the support, suggestions, and encouragement of Michael Galbraith and Mary Roberts at Krieger Publishing; the editing work of Barbara Scott and Don Hoyt; and the critiques and feedback from Elliott Garb, Marsha Rossiter, Carol Ryan, Robert Thompson and Carla Warner. A special thanks goes to Daniel Karis for his long hours of work on the index.

Our appreciation is also extended to our colleagues at the Department of Adult and Community College Education at North Carolina State University and the Department of Educational Psychology at University of Tennessee-Knoxville, and at the Department of Foundations and Adult Education at Kansas State University. The Office of Educational Research and Improvement of the U.S. Department of Education is also recognized for funding research support that led to many insights shared by the first author.

Although colleagues, practitioners and adult learners have

provided us critical assistance in writing this book, we recognize that without the support of our families and close friends we would not been able to sustain the energy and momentum needed to complete this book. Carol extends a special thanks to John Neill, her helpmate, whose care, support and love has been the beacon for those many moments of challenge in her life. Cheryl wishes to express her appreciation to her husband, Doug Polson, and her parents, Arnold and Rose Keller, who have always given confidence and support when she needed it most. Their loyalty, patience and love have inspired her more times than they know. Jane Fishback extends a thank-you to her daughters, Allison, Christina, and Joanna, because their continued commitment to her personal and professional growth is valued with love.

THE AUTHORS

Carol E. Kasworm is a professor and department head of Adult and Community College Education at North Carolina State University. She has also served on the faculty of the University of Tennessee-Knoxville, the University of Houston—Clear Lake, the University of Texas—Austin, and the University of South Florida. In addition, she has held administrative roles as associate vice chancellor for program and faculty development at the University of Houston—Clear Lake (a unique institution serving adult learners through upper division and master's programs), associate dean for research for the College of Education at the University of Tennessee-Knoxville, assistant director of housing at the University of Georgia, and resident instructor at the University of South Florida.

Her research on adult higher education has received a number of honors, including the Imogene Okes Research Award from the American Association for Adult and Continuing Education; the Outstanding Research Award from the Division of Research, National University Continuing Education Association; and the Helen B. Watson Outstanding Faculty Research Award from the College of Education, the University of Tennessee. In addition, she was awarded the 1996 Chancellor's Awards for Research and Creative Achievement by the University of Tennessee. She has two previous edited books, *Educational Outreach to Select Adult Populations* and *Revitalizing the Residential Conference Center Environment* (coauthored with E. Simpson.) Her recent contributions that focus on adult undergraduate students include writings in the *2000 Handbook of Adult and Continuing Education*, the *U.S. Higher Education Encyclopedia*, and the *International Encyclopedia of Education, Research and Studies*, as well as articles in *Research in Higher Education*,

Contemporary Education, Higher Education, Review of Educational Research, Adult Education, and other journals.

Cheryl J. Polson is currently a professor of Foundations and Adult Education and assistant dean of the Graduate School at Kansas State University. In addition to teaching, she directs three off-campus master's degree programs for adult learners. At Kansas State she has also served as director of an adult degree completion program and director of an academic advising center.

She has received numerous awards related to teaching, advising, publications, and professional service on behalf of adult learners. In 2000 she was the third recipient of the Excellence in Graduate Faculty Teaching Award from the College of Education at Kansas State. She has also received the Adult Educator of the Year Award from the Kansas Adult Education Association. She was selected by the Missouri Valley Adult Education Association as a recipient of its Achievement Award for her programming efforts on behalf of adult learners. Her commitment to quality academic advising was highlighted by her selection for the Outstanding Advisor Award by the National Academic Advising Association (NACADA). She also received a Certificate of Appreciation for Patriotic Civilian Service from the Department of the Army for her work with adult learners at the United States Command and General Staff College at Ft. Leavenworth, Kansas.

Known nationally for her work with adult learners, Cheryl was selected to serve on a national advisory panel for the development of a video-based academic advising training program. She was also selected as the recipient of the Contribution to the Literature Award given by the American College Personnel Association's Commission on Commuter Students and Adult Learners. Currently she is editor for the *Adult Learning* publication sponsored by the American Association for Adult and Continuing Education.

Sarah Jane Fishback is an assistant professor of Foundations and Adult Education at Kansas State University. Her research on adult learning in higher education received the outstanding graduate research award presented by the American College Personnel Association's Commission on Commuter Students and Adult Learners. She has given numerous presentations on adult cognitive development and the adult undergraduate experience at national conferences sponsored by the American Association for Adult and Continuing Educators, American College Personnel Association, National Association of Student Personnel Administrators, and the Midwest Research to Practice conference.

CHAPTER 1

Adult Students: Who Are They and Are They Different?

When I started college, I didn't know what I wanted to do, and so I dropped out. . . . As you mature, you realize that if you really want something, you're responsible and you're going to have to work for it. I lost my job last year—I was part of an expendable group of supervisors. After searching on the job market, I couldn't get a comparable job and salary without a degree. College will make a difference in my life; when I finish this degree, it can't be taken from me, and I can stand on equal footing in the job market. It is going to create a better future and one where I am more in control.—37-year-old adult student

I married quickly out of high school, and my dream shattered with the death of my husband. I had to quickly figure out how to support my kids and myself. But the work is hard and routine, and a part of me is slowly dying. I started college for me and for my kids . . . to create a better future for all of us, including a more financially stable life, where I can be productive. I need to grow in this world of changes, and I need to create a different sense of me. College is making that difference.—28-year-old adult student

I just retired last year. Although I had taken some college courses, I am now in here full-time so that I can learn about new and interesting things—getting my brain working in new ways. I'm not sure if I will pursue another career . . . but for now, I am having a ball being part of these young folks lives and becoming young again in spirit and mind. It's the best part of my life yet!—62-year-old adult student.

Being a college student does make a difference in an adult's life. It is a unique life commitment and set of experiences. Going to college doesn't come from parental demands, nor from the push and pull of friends and peers who want the student to be part of a party clique. It's not an opportunity to escape parental control, nor are adults attracted to a particular college because of heavy recruitment by collegiate institutions. Rather, adults seek out, enter, and participate in college because of their needs and their key life roles, and because they value collegiate knowledge for their future. College for adults is usually not the only commitment in their lives, nor is it typically a first-priority commitment. Adults have multiple work, family, and civic commitments, and often are the major providers and nurturers of others. They are responsible people in a responsible world, where college is often a valued effort based in discretionary time.

We often look at the adult through a single lens as a student participant within a collegiate setting; however, adult learners are first and foremost complex human beings. College is both a haven from and a valued stimulus for this complexity. It supports and challenges both the adult's sense of self and his or her sense of place. Some adults see college as a differing and sometimes colliding world in relation to their lives. For most, college is a rewarding commitment, providing significant joys and multiple rewards. And for some adults, college represents a place of anxiety and potential failure, a place of loneliness and ageism, and a place of insensitive bureaucracy.

To understand the adult learner in college, one needs to understand the diversity of adult learner characteristics, life environments, and emotional orientations. One must also come to understand the important dynamics of the collegiate cultures that attract, challenge, and often frustrate the adult learner. This chapter will provide a broad introductory overview of current national statistics and related research findings on adult college student characteristics. The last portion of this chapter will present suggested strategies for how to better define and profile adult students and their differing backgrounds and needs within an institution.

HOW ADULT UNDERGRADUATES ARE DIFFERENT: NATIONAL PERSPECTIVES

Although adult undergraduates are defined and considered differently because they are older, chronological age is just a

road marker, a societal perspective on life's journey. No key be-
haviors, characteristics, or understandings can be attributed
solely to a 21-year-old, versus a 30-year-old, versus a 50-year-old
student. Rather, research on adult development and learning
suggests that adults become increasingly different and complex
as individuals. Adult students do not have one set of common
characteristics. Instead, the common use of the "25-years-and-
older" age category to define adult students presents a practical way to separate and define a group of students who have
greater maturity, more complex life experiences, as well as more
significant heterogeneity and complexity than those who are
younger.

Many college administrators and researchers often define
adult undergraduate students as "nontraditional students." This
term is not used in these current discussions because the term
"nontraditional" can be applied to a wide variety of students
other than those who are over age 25. Nontraditional students
can also be younger students who are married, handicapped, ra-
cially or ethnically diverse, female, or part-time. In today's colleges, the vast majority of college students, both young and old,
are nontraditional by these standards. With these understandings regarding the nature of "adult" and "nontraditional" students, the next section will consider the current landscape of
adult undergraduate learners in college.

Collegiate Presence of Adult Students

The adult undergraduate student population, which includes students who are 25 or older, has increased dramatically—from 28% of all undergraduate students in 1971, to 41%
(including 24 and above) in 1991, to 35% (4.4 million) in 1997.
These changes represent both a recent increase in population
of high school graduates (both cohort size and growth of college entry), and a historic growth of adults seeking college enrollment. Looking across the landscape of collegiate institutions
in 1997 (NCES, 1995, 1996b, 1997), adult students reflected
22% of the population in public four-year and above institutions; 9.4% in four-year, private, not-for-profit institutions; and

8.3% in private for-profit institutions. Perhaps because of more flexible access and active cultural inclusion than four-year institutions, a larger representation of adult students attended regional institutions and community colleges, with adult students representing 58.7% of students at public two-year institutions. But the highest percentages of adult students typically choose specialized professional program institutions (often 60 to 75%) and specifically designed institutions for adult learners, which have 90% or higher adult student enrollment (Kasworm, 1995a). Practitioners recognize that institutional structures and programs targeted at adult access create the strongest adult participation. Thus, higher adult undergraduate student enrollments reflect one or more of the following characteristics:

- Colleges and academic programs geared to the part-time student, the evening and weekend student, the homemaker daytime student, and the geographically isolated adult student.
- Urban or regional campuses geared to workforce development, copartnerships with corporate universities, or to related community economic development efforts.
- Colleges and universities that have separate colleges or divisions for adult credit programs, such as evening schools, divisions of continuing education, or adult colleges designed for adult participation.
- Colleges and institutions that have supportive environments framed with adult-oriented academic policies, formats, curricula, and services, as well as external and internal recruitment, reward systems, and support systems for adults.
- Colleges and universities that offer alternative forms of prior assessment for academic equivalent experiences, such as the use of the College Level Examination Program (CLEP), College Credit Recommendation Services (CREDIT, formerly PONSI), local proficiency/challenge examinations, Defense Activity for Non-Traditional Education Support (DANTES), portfolios for life experiences equivalent to academic credit, and assessment mediums that assess knowledge and skill competency rather than seat-time credit hours for knowledge accumulation.
- Colleges and universities designed as upper-division institu-

tions—institutions that collaborate with regional community colleges and offer ease of access for the upper-division academic work.

- Colleges designed to serve adult students as the primary clientele—such as the historic adult mission institutions of Thomas Edison College, Regents College (now Excelsior College) and Empire State College; the burgeoning world of for-profit institutions such as the University of Phoenix; extensive external degree programs, such as Western Governor's University, Charter Oaks, and Atlanta Union College; and the related innovative technology-based degree programs, such as those offered through the University College at University of Maryland.
- Tribal colleges, which have dominantly served the adult learner.
- Community colleges and specialized professional academic institutions that provide specialized access and flexibility for adult learners and that often provide short-term learning experiences, such as certificate or degree-completion programs.

National Demographic Characteristics

Higher education has much to learn about the adult student population. The first focused monograph on national adult student demographics appeared in 1995, with many questions and curiosities still unexplored and unexplained. What is known about adult students? The following demographics come from the main sources of the National Center for Education Statistics (1995, 1996a, 1996b, 1997) and also represent information from Brickell (1995), Lamdin & Fugate, (1997), Kasworm (1990), Kasworm & Pike (1994), National University Continuing Education Association (1996), Tinto (1987), and Wallace (1979).

Adults represent meteoric growth in college enrollment and participation. The population of adult undergraduate college students (25 years of age or older) presents an amazing 171.4% increase from 1970 to 1991. The population of adult female students has experienced higher percentages of increase (59.2%) than the population of male adult students (40.8%). The most

Table 1.1. Comparative Statistics on Select Characteristics between Older and Younger Adult Undergraduates*

Comparative Status of	Percentage of Older Students (25 years and older)	Percentage of Younger Students (under 25 years)
Part-Time Course Load	69%	27%
Full-time Workers & Part-time Students	55%	36%
Full-time Worker and Full-time student	23%	23%
Married or Separated	56%	6.5%
Dependent Children	52%	3.9%
First-generation college student	55%	44%
Financial aid to all students	39%	44%
Grant Support	34%	36%
Loans	15%	21%
Employer Aid	9%	1%
Full-time student financial aid support	71%	41%
African American student representation	11.1%	8.7%

*Note - Percentages come from a variety of studies, from a variety of years, and slightly differing definitions of older and younger student groupings.

significant percentage of change in enrollment has occurred in the number of women who are 35 years of age and older, with a 500% growth in enrollment between 1970 and projected year 2000. The projected number of adult undergraduates for the year 2000, 6.3 million, will be equivalent to the total enrollment of all undergraduate and graduate American college students in 1966.

All adult age groups have shown enrollment growth. Over the last 30 years, substantial growth has occurred in college enrollments for the 35-years-and-older age range with a 248.8% increase (823,000 in 1971 to 2,867,000 in 1997). Two other age groups of adult students also have experienced significant growth rates: The 30-to-34-year-old group had a 201.4% increase during that same time frame (487,000 to 1,468,000), and the 25-to-29-year-old student group had a 98.8 % increase (1,074,000 to 2,135,000). With the graying of society, the number of adults who are 60 years of age and older has steadily increased. In 1997, these adults constituted 6% of the current undergraduate collegiate enrollments. Depending upon both collegiate policies and societal support for senior adult learners, this age group may well be a new service challenge for American higher education.

Adult students currently represent ethnic and racial percentages of enrollment that are somewhat similar to those of younger college students. Racial and ethnicity differences do not appear to be unique deterrents for adults enrolling in college. Of special interest is the fact that African American adult undergraduates represent a higher percentage of enrollments in college (11.1%) than younger African American undergraduates (8.7%).

Adult students typically have major family responsibilities. Approximately 56% of adult undergraduate students are married or separated, in comparison to 6.5% of younger undergraduates. Fifty two percent (52%) have one or more dependent children in comparison to 3.9% of younger students. Of special significance, approximately 21% of female adult undergraduates are single parents. Moreover, although the number is not yet statistically documented, many adult students often face special responsibilities for semi-dependent aging parents.

Adult students are more likely to be part-time college students. Approximately 69% of adult undergraduates versus 27% of younger students carry less than half a collegiate course load each term.

Adult students are more likely to combine full-time work with collegiate studies. Approximately half of adult undergraduate students are full-time workers who work 40 or more hours a week. One-quarter of adult students hold jobs for 20 to 39 hours a week, and the remaining one-quarter work less than 20 hours a week. Although 55% of adult undergraduates are full-time workers and part-time students, increasing numbers of younger undergraduates (36%) work full-time and participate in part-time collegiate studies. Although adult students are often perceived as over-committed to both work and collegiate study, equivalent percentages (approximately 23%) of both adult and younger students attend college full-time and engage in full-time employment.

Adults are more likely to be first-generation college attendees. The majority of adult undergraduate students have parents who were not college attendees. Fifty-five percent of adult students versus 44% of younger undergraduates reflect first-generation attendance.

Adults are more likely to come from lower socioeconomic backgrounds. In comparison with younger students, adult undergraduates typically have backgrounds reflecting family incomes of $27,000 a year or less.

Adults are more likely to be reentry students and to have experienced other collegiate institutions and academic programs. In studies of select adult student institutional participation patterns at four-year institutions in 1992–94, just 10% of undergraduate adults were "native" students who had never enrolled in another collegiate institution and had been continuously enrolled in degree pursuits. The vast majority of adult undergraduates (approximately 70% to 90%) were reentry adults (as defined by previous enrollments in other institutions or who had not been continuously enrolled since the first term of their freshmen year). Depending upon the institution's location and its policies and programs, many adult students bring three to four transcripts from other institutions to integrate into a current program of studies.

Adult students have a different resource base for financing college attendance. Slightly fewer adult undergraduates received external financial aid (39% adults versus 44% younger students) for college attendance in a 1989–90 Postsecondary Financial Aid Study. These financial supports included grants (34% for adult students and 36% for young students), loans (15% for adults and 21% for young students), and employer aid (9% for adults with 1% for young students). One important difference occurred in the financial support for full-time adult students. These students gain greater access to higher aid support, with 71% receiving some form of aid (as compared to 51% of younger

full-time undergraduates). The breakdown of these higher percentages represent grants (with 62% of older adult undergraduates versus 44% of younger students receiving grants), loans
(43% for adult undergraduates versus 27% for younger), and
employer aid (2% for adult versus 0.5% for younger students).

**Adult students report their highest issue and most stressful
concern is their financial fragility in supporting college attendance.** Because adult students are often the key financial supporters of themselves and their families, college funding comes
from either renegotiated family funds, from commitments to
loans, or from limited institutional and federal financial supports. As noted above, employer support for college participation is limited. Paying for a college education for most adults
means negotiating family and personal financial needs each semester with college tuition, class costs, and commuting costs.

**Adults represent a major subgroup of disabled college stu-
dents.** In a recent update on collegiate students with disablities
in 1999, approximately 50% of collegiate disabled undergraduates were 30 years of age or older, with 25% representing 40
years of age or older. This figure seems rather unusual until one
realizes that a college education is often an important vehicle
for adults who have had major life transitions. Adults seek out
college as an alternative after facing medical or other life crises
and subsequent disabilities. They view college as an important
second life opportunity to becoming financially independent
and a productive worker.

Academic Characteristics

**Adult students receive similar, if not higher, grade point
averages in comparison to young students.** Adult undergraduate
students do as well as, if not academically better than, their
younger counterparts. These findings have been substantiated
from many studies considering different adult subgroupings,
different academic fields, different institutional settings, and
different decades of collegiate participation by adult students
(Kasworm, 1990; Kasworm & Pike, 1994). These studies have

often incorporated varied predictive models of academic achievement. In all of the studies, the majority of adult students were academically successful in college.

Adult college freshmen typically enter college with lower high school grade-point averages and lower class rankings in high school. Adult freshmen reflect a small subset of the adult student population, yet they are often a uniquely important target group for college recruitment. They are higher risk students because they often bring limited college prep coursework from their high school backgrounds. This is partially offset, however, as identified by one study (Solomon & Gordon, 1981), wherein approximately 24% of older freshmen had taken previous college courses. In another study of adult freshmen at a regional four-year institution, approximately 15% had recently completed their GED (General Equivalency Diploma). In the Kasworm and Blowers study (1994), most entering adult freshmen who had targeted their initial goal of success as a two-year degree, were unemployed or semiskilled workers. In contrast, most adult freshmen who had a goal of a four-year degree were pursuing professional or administrative careers and were enrolled in a four-year college.

Adult students reflect uneven prior academic subject preparation when compared to younger students. Adult students bring varied knowledge and skill backgrounds to college studies. In studies during the 1970s and 1980s, adult undergraduates scored higher on humanities exams than younger students; had similar scores to younger undergraduates in English, written expression, social science, and natural science; and scored substantially lower on algebra and quantitative skills tests. In more recent studies, a greater percentage of adults than younger students entering or reentering college reported a higher level of concern about rusty skills or lack of academic background knowledge in mathematics and algebra. Adults also noted greater concern for improving study skills than younger students, particularly retention of academic memorized knowledge, effective written expression in academic papers and test essays, and test-taking skills in multiple-choice and short-answer essay tests.

Adults report higher levels of satisfaction with their academic experience in comparison with younger students. In a number of studies, adult undergraduates report greater satisfaction with the quality of their educational experience than younger students, in particular with the academic aspects of their education (such as advising, courses, and instruction).

Adults participate in a variety of credit course offerings beyond the collegiate campus. Adult undergraduates participate in collegiate learning in a variety of learning environments and formats. In a recent report of *Lifelong Learning Trends* (National University Continuing Education Association, 1996), 11 million adults completed college and university-based credential courses; only a part of this group represented the approximately 6.5 million adults who are 25 years of age or older enrolled in college credit programs. Of those adult undergraduates who were pursuing credential education, the majority (60%) took courses provided by business or professional associations. About 20% took work-related courses provided by colleges, and 17% took work-related courses provided by governmental agencies.

Although these national demographic figures and related institutional research studies provide an important awareness of the complexity and patterns of adult undergraduates, collegiate leaders recognize that each institution's adult learner population is unique due to programs and structures that attract adult students and because of regional demographics and the workforce activities of adult students. To attract and retain adult students, each institution needs to understand the who, what, and why of the adult student population. This understanding comes from four strategies for developing both campus and program profiles of adult students.

DEVELOPING A CAMPUS PROFILE: BEST PRACTICES FOR IDENTIFYING OPPORTUNITIES AND CHALLENGES

How do college administrators come to know their institution's adult learners and what they need and value in a college experience? Unlike young students who have certain commonalties (recent high school graduation, young adult years, and no prior collegiate experience), adult students bring unique and sometimes highly complex life sagas with their entry. In attempting to understand and serve adult students, college administrators need to identify both common characteristics and differing subgroupings of adult students and also the varied processes that engage and support the individual needs of adults.

Most colleges rely heavily upon select faculty and staff perceptions of adult students to guide policy and services. As valuable as these observations and experiences are, often these faculty and staff experience only a small subset of adult students. Many adult students will purposefully seek out assistance only for problems they believe the college can solve. And many adults will find alternative ways to solve their college concerns because they may see the institution as a generically elitist, bureaucratic, or youth-oriented structure. Furthermore, most colleges and universities don't have a single place or set of staff to serve all adult learners as they progress through the institution. The challenge is to create within the institution a number of needs assessment and data collection activities—both to paint a general profile and to delineate select characteristics of adult students. The following four strategies are commonly used.

Admissions and Institutional Learner Profiles

Collegiate institutions serve adults by rethinking the primary information needed for selecting adult students in the admission process, for documenting student demographic characteristics, for planning curriculum and support services, and for institutional effectiveness. Many college administrators believe their student population reflects a continuum of backgrounds and characteristics most often highlighted by the diversity of adult students.

Practitioners leading institutional change are rethinking the initial collection of admissions data and related efforts both to identify essential characteristics of students and to provide initial contact information for recruitment. Depending upon in-

stitutional needs for admissions selection and institutional pro-
filing, primary areas of data needs include (a) prior educational
background, including prior college attendance and need for
transcript evaluation and advisement; (b) work experiences and
involvements, such as employer and job title as well as work
schedules; (c) family status, including dependents and potential
demands for child care; (d) professional and personal leadership
and citizenship involvements through work and community
(often used for adult degree program admission); and (e) other
information important to the nature of the institution and the
region. Many institutions have multiple sections on admissions
forms to serve the entry high school senior and their characteristics and needs, and another section for adult learners with
other important information as noted above.

Adult-oriented colleges and universities have specific admissions policies to reflect adult student backgrounds. For example,
institutions with adult admissions policies request submission of
an alternative statement of proficiency and competency through
a resume of work, family, and community-related activities, and
leadership roles. Whether it be part of admissions or orientation,
some adult degree programs require students to provide an educational biography both to ascertain past education involvements and to understand the adult's beliefs about learning and
formal schooling. These information resources also create an excellent basis for developing profiles and cluster group characteristics of adult students.

Personal Interviews and Interactions

Adult-oriented collegiate environments usually have a variety of ways to make contact and get updated information on
their adult college students. Many institutions have established
specific entry or reentry orientation programs, initial screening
interviews, or other introductory and advisement experiences
for adult students. Although these entry or reentry events often
become a monologue of information about the institution and
its services, they also should reflect opportunities for adult stu-

dents to voice needs related to their initial goals and plans for collegiate participation. More important, these contacts can provide significant data regarding the uniqueness of the student, participation strategies, and student needs.

Initial personal discussions, whether they be individual or group interviews, provide excellent information for understanding the adult student and for planning targeted services. From the staff member's perspective, a protocol listing of pertinent questions is often a helpful device for these personal contacts. These questions could include the following:

- Why have you chosen to enter or reenter college?
- What are your past and current college enrollment experiences?
- What is your preferred academic major, and what are the limitations for your access to specific curricula or classes, as well as potential needs for career counseling information?
- What is your work status, and what are your goals?
- What is your current family status, and what are your support systems?
- Do you have particular concerns related to academic study skills, time management, and test-taking?
- Do you have specific concerns of a personal or social nature in relation to college?

At these interview sessions, adult students usually come with specific questions and needs. Staff members need to provide sufficient time for adults to explore issues, share interests and concerns with other adult students, and receive a variety of resource assistance. Not all adults, however, are seekers of all information; some adults are very time-conscious and knowledge savvy. They don't want to waste their time at another "orientation event." In one study (Kasworm & Blowers, 1994), just 35% of the adult students at four-year institutions reported attending voluntary orientation meetings. Thus, staff need to be mindful that adults self-select the programs they participate in and the information they reveal. One staff member in an office for nontraditional students noted that she predominantly saw adults who needed academic intervention, career counseling, or special institutional resources. Her primary involvement with these adult students probably reflected about 10% of the college's adult students and perhaps a skewed set of issues. To gain a broader perspective, this staff member was very purposeful about alternative ways to gain adult student interviews to balance out her drop-in and appointment-based interviews.

Personal interactions have been an important source for understanding the complexity of adult students. A few programs are experimenting with initial planning discussions with adults. These discussions include asking the adults to present their current planning for activities they believe will help them to be successful at college; how they will handle work, family, and community commitments that may thwart their attendance; and how they will create supports for studying, library research, and writing papers. Often these planning discussions create a helpful base for dialogues with college personnel about future college assistance for these students, as well as helping them with personal and academic advising. These personal discussions also could suggest changes in the community that bring adults back to the college. For example, in the last number of years, college staff have experienced the impact of Welfare-to-Work reforms on adults and their college attendance. Likewise, recent business closures creating dislocated workers, changing financial aid requirements, and regional businesses pushing workers towards collegiate credentialling or certification for new specialties have affected adult student enrollments.

Personal interviews provide clear voices and pictures of the solved and the unsolved issues facing adult students. And each adult presents specialized life circumstances that makes the resolution of these issues often a unique intervention rather than a "one-solution-works-for-all" approach. Understanding adult students through these personal contacts means coming to know them as individuals—their life stories, their concerns, and their aspirations for the future. More significantly, adult students also gain from these personal interactions. Through these contacts, they create a set of beliefs about the institution, its support, and its valuing of adults. Savvy adult students quickly pick up on institutional and staff concerns and their awareness of the students' relative importance in the institution.

Demographic Survey Studies

Many adult student services offices, adult programs, and adult-oriented colleges have considered and implemented varied forms of demographic surveys either to recruit or to better serve current adult students. These surveys may be directed to either current or prospective adult students and may focus upon global information or more specific interests in academic formats, course scheduling, policy-related concerns, or support service needs. Demographic surveys can offer a refined understanding of both adult student characteristics and their participation patterns, as well as met and unmet perceived needs. These types of surveys have proven most helpful in identifying primary characteristics, which are frequently necessary due to the lack of adequate admissions and institutional data reflecting adult learner characteristics. For example, most institutions would value the demographics of an adult's family, information about an individual's work and community commitments, a profile of the main services he or she uses on campus, and information about the individual's other needs as an adult student. With the push towards assessment, surveys can prove extremely valuable for identifying subgroupings of adults and for clarifying types of adult student use and satisfaction with current campus services and support systems. Demographic and support service surveys provide greatest value when they are tailored to the particular institutional context of programs, services, policies, and adult populations.

One early example of a demographic survey is the *Adult Learner Needs Assessment Survey* and the *ACT Student Profile Report* from American College Testing Program. Few institutions, however, report current use of this survey instrument. Another early survey, the *Survey of Student Needs*, was used by Mangano and Corrado (1980) in their research with the New

York system. These types of surveys offer helpful information about the particular needs and interests of adult students. Practitioners that currently use these survey instruments, however, suggest that their greatest strength is in looking at subgroupings of students within the data. For example, who are the individuals who have a need for and interest in child care or in orientation? Which types of adults have stated an interest in study skills development or remedial courses for basic skills? A number of institutions have used the American Council on Education's resource, *Focus on Adults—A Self-Study Guide for Postsecondary Educational Institutions* (2001). This resource offers a variety of helpful inventories for assessing academic and student planning and services.

Although it is difficult initially to develop and administer a survey to adult students, many programs have found value in a customized survey. These customized surveys provide specific context questions, speak to specific academic and support services, and often can provide a better understanding of representative adult student groupings than standardized surveys. Those who desire to develop and administer such a survey instrument need to identify knowledgeable people to create the survey either through their institutional research office, through select faculty who have survey development expertise, or through their own ingenuity. Designing, administering, and disseminating the results of a survey is best orchestrated by a planning group of individuals across both academic and student affairs services. Ideally, the survey would have top academic and student affairs support, as well as funding. In addition, long-term planning is required to readminister the survey in three to five years for trend analysis. Surveys of adult students have been conducted in the last 15 years by many institutions, including those offices responsible for adult student services at the University of North Carolina—Charlotte and University of Tennessee—Knoxville.

Adults can be notorious about not responding to surveys, unless they view this effort as producing a favorable impact upon themselves or others like them. Ways to get better responses include piloting the instrument, considering the design for clarity and a professional look, limiting the length for a response time of under 20 minutes, linking to potential new programs or support for adults, distributing at a time when adults are more likely to act on the request, and having the response linked to some form of reward. (For example, one program offered a $100 support for books using a lottery system for received responses.) In addition, survey developers should contact the Undergraduate Returning Students Program Data Bank at the University of Maryland at College Park. This data base provides a number of institutional projects related to surveys and other forms of data collection.

Demographic surveys are often assumed to be for the entire adult student population. Many institutions may elect an alternative related to enrollment in special programs, attendance at a particular time of day (daytime versus evening) or a weekend, or the selection of a stratified sample. Some institutions have worked with their regional key industrial companies and their human resources offices regarding surveys of workers with college interests and involvements. A few institutions have experimented with newspaper advertisements, including data collection through published contact numbers, community interest meetings, or Web-based offerings for interested responses. Although these efforts are not as helpful for defining the totality of an institution's adult student population, they do provide select data for and connections with prospective, if not current, clusters of adult students.

Focus Group or Phone Interview Sampling

Institutions committed to adult undergraduate students have found that focus group or phone interviews can prove extremely beneficial. Often these focus groups or phone interviews provide an alternative to the demographic survey and personal discussions on campus. As with the demographic survey, these data collection efforts depend upon appropriate sampling strategies, as well as appropriately developed questions and data collection methods. For example, to establish an in-depth understanding, one type of interview concentrates on the academic life history of the adult. This elongated baseline interview centers on information about how one entered the institution, what was helpful and what was not, how one is currently using the institution, how one is accessing or not accessing services and supports, and how the institution may connect or not connect with the adult student. Another type of focus group or phone interview specifically targets a particular aspect of concern: the academic curriculum, recruitment strategies, needs for and satisfaction with support services, potential outreach workshops or written resource supports, and other specialized topics of interest. For example, many institutions remain concerned about student retention, recognizing that access and support from admissions, registrar and registration, advisement, faculty resources, financial aids, and the library do make a difference. One example reported by staff at National Louis University used focus groups for an undergraduate management program (Ashar & Lane, 1993). With the changing work world, some institutions have found it valuable to conduct group discussions on adult-oriented placement and career development services, tutoring and special basic skills tutoring, and other targeted services such as an office for reentry and nontraditional students that serves adult students.

Because of the intensive staff time invested in these efforts, the program personnel who conduct these specialized efforts will often purposefully select a specific group. These efforts may look at a particular cluster group of adults (such as those who only attend evening, weekend, or daytime courses) or emphasize particular areas of concern such as orientation, curriculum, or distance delivery. For maximum impact, one college has included select staff and faculty in these focus groups as "listening posts" to these discussions. Effectively capturing and reframing the information for other faculty or staff can be difficult. These individuals aided the adult student advocate in defining essential information, concerns, and action possibilities. Data that sits on a shelf collecting dust is not helpful! Each of these efforts must be carefully designed to enhance future dissemination of important findings and to have impact upon key people and appropriate policy groups.

HOW TO COME TO KNOW ADULT STUDENTS

This chapter has suggested ways for practitioners to anchor their understanding of adult students in national and institutional demographic data, as well as to develop an institutional database to define both global and specific adult student profiles. The challenge is to design an ongoing data resource to be both helpful and communicative to college decision-makers—such as academic policy and curriculum planners, student support service staff, and college outreach programs—and to support one's own planning and implementation of adult student resource support. Global institutional demographic information can be an important first level of understanding; it is usually necessary, however, to identify major adult student subgroupings by their types of involvement and participation, and by the particular needs that could be served by the institution and possibly the community. In addition, regional, family, or work factors unrelated to the institution influence many adults in their college participation. To come to understand the complex participation of adults, the staff members need to be tuned into the external world of adult life through interactions with employers and nonprofit agencies as well as through dialogues with other practitioners at other postsecondary institutions who also serve adult students. What information should motivate the actions of chief advocates for adult students in higher education institutions? Key questions to be asked include the following:

• What does the institution currently know about its adult students?
• What does the institution need to know to recruit, serve, and graduate adult students?
• What specific programs, services, and resources are crucial to adult participation?
• Which staff and faculty will be pivotal leaders in this adult student assessment?
• How will the collected data be used for planning and action?

CHAPTER 2

Recruiting and Retaining Adult Students: What Is Important to Them?

I always was going to do my college degree, but my family comes first. I wanted a place close by, courses that fit my schedule in the mornings, and one that would be supportive of me as an adult and as a mother of young children. I want to show my children that education is important.—31 year-old student

I want to get the best degree possible, so I chose this university because it is prestigious. My degree will be special. I will have the best professors and the most challenging learning environment. Yes, I have to negotiate with my work regarding specific classes, but it's the best education. It also will show my parents that they will get their dream. I dropped out of college when I was young, and I promised them that I would finish one day—they sacrificed a lot.—34 year-old student

At this point, I want a college and degree program that is a customized adult learning environment, offered at a time and place that fits my work schedule. I just don't want to deal with the Mickey Mouse stuff of other colleges. I want a degree that directly relates to what I am doing in my supervisory position, so that I can get ahead. I want to be in classes with other adults like me who understand the urgency of getting the knowledge and its immediate application to work.—37 year-old student

One of an educator's greatest challenges is understanding these adult perspectives and their influence on collegiate involvement. To serve adult learners thoughtfully, educators first need to understand that adult students come from a different place, with different needs, and with concerns that are both similar to and different from those of younger students. This chapter will speak to adult beliefs about the entry or reentry process and the actions they motivate, as well as the factors that influence adult persistence.

RETHINKING COLLEGE ATTENDANCE
THROUGH AN ADULT'S EYES

Most college leaders think of undergraduate studies as a young adult experience, a cultural oasis for young adult intellectual and psychological development. With this image, many collegiate administrators and faculty have difficulty conceiving of adults as undergraduate students. And often adult students also believe that undergraduate studies and the college campus are for the young, the brave, and the gifted. They question how they will "fit in." They wonder if the college will accept and value them as students. Adults believe that college is a special place, a special culture. They are concerned because they view college as an elite place with very special demands. They recognize that they are different because they experience college as an interconnected experience within their larger world, rather than an isolated island of living and learning. They must incorporate college studies into a full and responsible life of work, family, and community.

As noted in Chapter 1, these adult students make up a diverse group, often representing growing segments of part-timers, commuters, and "college mobile" reentry students who bring three or four transcripts of prior college work to their current college experience. Because adults have such heterogeneous needs, life circumstances, and variable patterns of college attendance, recruiting and retaining them becomes a complex process. Understanding this process includes considering adult motives and goals, influences on adult collegiate entry, and related influences on their subsequent continuation.

ADULT MOTIVES AND GOALS
FOR ATTENDANCE

A highly complex set of motives and goals influences each adult learner's decision to enroll. For most adults, college attendance can create new opportunities—a credential, access to a new job, a promotion, personal development, or economic life security. In most research studies and personal conversations, adult students voice their primary goals for college attendance as pointing toward a career or job situation, such as preparing for a first career, a career change, or career enrichment, as well as improving their family's financial future. They also usually note, however, second and third motives or goals that are expressive rather than pragmatic. Many adults also suggest that they are seeking an enhanced or different identity; others desire to bring closure to previous life commitments by completing a college degree program. Some view college attendance as personal intellectual enrichment, as a way to become an educated person and to contribute to the betterment of society by gaining new knowledge. And a few enter college confused, hoping that their involvement in college will give them new insights and understandings, new tools to create a better life, and special assistance with figuring out how they can reshape themselves for a new future.

Initial Motivators for Entry

What causes adults to enter college? Whereas young adult students are motivated to enter college as the next life step after high school, adults come with more diverse motivators. Adults enroll in college due to (a) personal transitions and changes, (b) proactive life planning, or (c) a mixture of both personal transition and proactive planning.

Personal Transitions and Changes

Many adults enroll in college because of major life transitions and changes. These personal transitions motivate them to seek out college because they have new and personal understandings with which to act on college pursuits, or they may feel external pressures to get a college degree. Researchers have found that most adults enroll in college based upon these personal life transition opportunities (Aslanian & Brickell, 1980;

Sewall, 1984). In the 1980 study, 56% of adults noted career transition as a key trigger, 16% reported family-related triggers, and 13% noted leisure-related triggers. The remaining individuals noted esthetic- or art-related transitions (5%), health-related transitions (5%), religion- or spiritual-related transitions (4%) and citizenship- or societal-related triggers (1%). These personal catalysts reflect environmental forces, life changes, or external events. For example, adults may enter college because of a divorce, children entering school, or a spouse completing college. Some adults may enter because of a recent job loss or a physical disability that forces them to consider new work options, while others may experience being denied job promotion due to the lack of a college degree.

For these adults, initial information contacts with colleges and related staff and faculty have a major impact on entry. Orientation and related support services information often prove to be essential influences on persistence, as does strong academic advisement support. Often these adults have not fully considered the long-term view of attending college and the changes they will need to make in their current life to be successful in college. They view college as a means to an end—to their future life status—rather than on the collegiate journey. They may have unrealistic or idealized beliefs about college's impact on their future careers. Some will desire a swift pace through college studies, thereby seeking unrealistic courseloads; others may assume that emotional support will be readily accessible through college staff and faculty as they deal with significant personal life changes and related emotional turbulence. Often these individuals desire special intervention programs to aid them in exploring themselves and these transitions, as well as to help them gain awareness, knowledge, and alternative resources for guiding their futures. Workshops or seminars for career exploration and testing, special daytime programs for women in transition, and special workshops for employees facing job loss all become valuable supports. In addition, a few colleges have developed divorce or family support groups and personal development seminars geared to adult students.

Proactive Life Planning

While the adults who enter college because of life transitions react to their world and are often responsive to change or dramatically pushed into it, this second group is purposeful and proactive about creating change by seeking a new world of opportunities. Through beliefs about self-destiny and life planning, these adults seek new life choices that will provide greater benefits and rewards than their current situations. For example, many adults recognize that their life is static and at a dead-end or that they are living an unstable and unpredictable life. In dealing with these discomforts, they seek out college studies to make a life change. They often start from a process of personal comparative appraisal with others or develop an ideal image for their future. Through reflection and active information collection, these adults come to value future collegiate participation and see it as a vehicle to reshape or enhance their lives.

In Kasworm and Blowers's 1994 research, many interviewed adult students were proactive planners who sought out college studies after several years of thinking about college and examining information sources. Many noted that they waited for family circumstances to change, such as a spouse completing a degree or children reaching a certain life stage. Others noted either seeking a new community for relocation so they could gain access to a particular type of college, seeking employment from a company with a tuition reimbursement plan, or seeking changes in work load or travel commitments to support college studies. Others sought out new financial resources or procured a significant other's support for this commitment.

The individuals in this group can be identified by their determination to understand the collegiate system and how to succeed as students. They ask many questions related to curricula, course scheduling, and acceptance of past coursework into current curricula. And these individuals scrutinize the catalog and any collegiate literature regarding policies and procedures. They plan and negotiate their future; they want to know, be efficient, and have control of their future. A portion of these adults will seek out degree programs that can assure them of course scheduling to meet their needs (often adult degree programs), that will provide remedial or tutorial support for their initial deficiencies (community colleges), or that will provide access to cooperative education experiences for career changes (universities). These individuals are also more likely than other adult learners to seek out external degree, distance learning, or specialized instructional scheduling to support their complex adult lifestyles because of rotating shift work, extensive travel schedules, or rural location. These students also may not have the best skills in planning and execution. Thus, college staff and faculty will hear these learners express clear commitments to their goals and plans; college personnel, however, may need to suggest strategies, provide further goal exploration, and encourage these students to gain advanced understanding about balancing course and life loads as they realistically face their future as students.

Mixed Motivators of Both Personal Transition and Proactive Planning

A third group of adults begins or resumes college studies in response to both sets of motivators: personal life transitions and external pressures as well as proactive planning of goals and life priorities for college studies. Although Kasworm and Blowers's study revealed that the adult students who fell into this third group were quite diverse, those who had reentered college and attended for a year or more often fit this mixed motivator orientation. Their current goals and motives reflected change and were more complex than their earlier beliefs about single motivations for pursuing college. At this juncture in their lives, they saw themselves identifying three to six life transition and proactive goals for college participation (Kasworm & Blowers, 1994).

Another group of adult students with this mixed motive set were partially influenced to enroll in college by societal messages and power relationships between themselves and their world (Kasworm & Blowers, 1994; Quinnan, 1997). For example, some adults viewed college attendance as achieving societal self-worth; they believed that a college degree conferred upon them prestige and a higher social class standing. These adult students suggested that they felt excluded in a variety of social gatherings and conversations with their work colleagues who held a college degree. Some adults felt that they had disappointed parents who had earlier supported their initial college enrollment; they wanted to change their status as college dropouts. Others felt that the work environment only valued and promoted college graduates. Thus, these adults were seeking a college degree to rectify these perceptions, to gain more personal power and prestige, and to respond to a culture that placed heavy emphasis upon credentials and collegiate learning.

Acting on Adult Motives and Goals

It is imperative that staff, faculty, and peer mentors to adult students identify and understand these complexities and changes in adult goals and motives at a personal level. At an institutional level, these diverse goals and motives should be reflected through recruitment messages and strategies, in initial orientation literature and entry support programs, and in academic program structures and advisement.

Adults in personal transition often need supportive advisement and services for a nurturing and facilitating entry experience. In addition, faculty and staff need to provide opportunities for adults to develop an understanding of alternative actions and resources for their college participation. If individuals are making a lifestyle choice, they want to be assured that they will succeed and be able to reach their goals, and that the program, the courses, and the process will stay in place while they complete their studies. If they are experiencing life transitions, they need to have collegiate staff and resources to help them balance this life change with the realities of college academic demands. (Refer to Chapter 4 in this book for further information about academic advising and specific advising strategies.)

Although many adults enter with confidence and self-assurance, many others are unsure of themselves, question their abilities to compete in an academic environment, and sometimes lack

a strong, unwavering commitment to this long journey toward
degree completion. Many adult students seek validation of their
worth and success as adult students through the initial admissions process and their first visits to the campus offices and academic departments, and through services for adults. They also
carefully monitor faculty responsiveness, as well as their own
performance, during the first class session with faculty, in course
feedback and subsequent end-of-course grades, and through interactions with academic advisors. Similar to young adults, these
adult attendees sometimes have wavering courage and diminished belief in themselves, and therefore limited emotional resources to support persistence in college. These individuals present a particularly important challenge for staff, faculty, and the
collegiate environment. They need to be supported, validated,
and honored with dignity. As staff and faculty examine their
interactions, services, and programs for adults, they should consider

- actions that provide support for life transition changes in
  adult lives,
- actions that validate adults' worth and value as entering students,
- actions that provide information and resources to support
  adults,
- actions that provide planning and structure for adult access,
  and
- actions that encourage adults to continue this important journey.

DYNAMICS OF DECISION MAKING
FOR PARTICIPATION

Although the decision to enter college is a major change in
an adult's life, there are also important dynamics that influence
the continued enrollment and participation of adult students.
This section will explore those forces that influence adult persistence.

Key Decision-Making Forces

Just as the motives for and goals of college entry are highly complex and diverse, the ongoing decision-making process of participation is also beyond easy explanation or prediction. Adult students continually find themselves enmeshed in complex, dynamic decision forces. Once adults initially enroll in college, they don't automatically stay enrolled. Each semester they experience significant pushes and pulls from many corners of their world and within themselves. They negotiate and renegotiate internal and external expectations related to their many duties and responsibilities. At least 30% of adult students in one study had to specifically consider whether they could continue their enrollment for each upcoming semester (Kasworm & Blowers, 1994). Adult students find that their goals and motives for college attendance are tested, supported, and sometimes diminished by both the collegiate world and their other worlds. As part of multiple communities and relationships, adult students have many hidden collaborators who may act as partners in their academic adventure or they may have hidden saboteurs who disrupt their college involvement. These decision-making forces for continued participation usually involve five essential areas of self and society that are depicted in Figure 2.1.

Work Responsibilities

Work roles are often reported as one of the strongest forces in college persistence. Adult workers believe their economic livelihood, their job, and future employment are paramount to their day-to-day survival. As responsible financial providers for their families, adult students view work as pivotal to a stable adult life. This concept of work responsibilities can also be translated into important childcare provider roles. Whether adult students are Supermoms or Mister Moms, whether they are single parents or the primary person who supervises children in a family, the welfare of raising and supervising children takes as much prominence as an externally paid work role. These adult work roles define possibilities for commitment and access to college

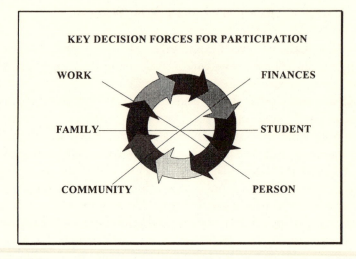

Figure 2.1.

studies. These work roles also can provide support for college studies, including financing.

For effective adult participation, staff and faculty should consider ways to engage employers to support college enroll- ment, whether through specialized program arrangements or through college career day fairs with employers. Newspaper and college information brochures that highlight the accomplish- ments of working students who complete degree programs and who make an impact on their work environments have proven to be helpful. A few colleges conduct outcome assessments with their adult student employers and receive valuable feedback and support. And faculty and staff can actively support, value, and use each learner's work experiences within collegiate learning experiences through courses, peer interactions, and counseling workshops.

Family and Significant Other Responsibilities

The second influence on adult decisions involves family roles. Most adult students have primary responsibility for sup- porting and nurturing personal relationships with their spouses, their children, their parents, and significant others. And most adult students believe they can be most successful as students with understanding, support, and involvement from these individuals. Significant research on spousal and family support and conflict demonstrates the strong impact made by relationships and roles on adults' sense of confidence, their commitment to college studies, and their persistence. As shown in the film *Educating Rita*, there are husbands who do burn the college texts of their college-bound spouses and threaten further abuse, and there are wives who present significant guilt and hardship to husbands attending evening college programs. Even in the most supportive family situations, adult students often need to redefine and renegotiate family role expectations and to rethink time commitments to family relationships.

College faculty and staff need to identify ways of making the campus a family-oriented environment. Can orientation also be held for families of adult students, similar to parents' orientation for traditional-age students? Can a college's student activities program include a family night movie series? What about college classrooms allowing an occasional visit from children to see the work of their parents? Can college personnel offer workshops for adult students and their families related to renegotiating the student role and the family role?

Financial Responsibilities

Entering and participating in college involves special financial issues for adult students. This influencer reflects both the adult's need to maintain a financial support structure for self and family while also seeking additional financial support for college studies. Adults face problems because of the lack of clear and consistent financial support for college studies through the college and the government. Few scholarships target adult students, and adults rarely qualify for sufficient financial aid. A limited number of employers provide tuition reimbursement plans, and those companies often support selective college degree programs or coursework. More often than not, the adult must first consider family discretionary income as a primary source for college funding and then hope for funds from other sources. This precarious situation is common to most adult students for each semester of their participation. In one group of adults, these financial issues create a special stop-out and come-back pattern: These adults endure a cycle of saving discretionary funds for enrollment and then attending college until the funds are spent.

College staff and faculty rarely look for ways to ameliorate the financial concerns of adult students. A few institutions, however, have sought special adult student scholarships or stipends for books and course materials, established emergency rainy day loan funds for adults, and created special child care support resources for adult students. A few institutions also have developed information literature to aid adults in understanding the resources and options that they may have in planning for financial support to attend college.

Community Responsibilities

The fourth area of influence involves each adult's contributory role in the community. Many adults bring past and present civic leadership and service to their college experience. Adults often find, however, that these time commitments are the most vulnerable to being reduced or eliminated when they enter college. Of equal concern, whether an adult has been a leader in a civic organization, an active supporter of PTA, or a voluntary contributor to Habitat for Humanity, his or her involvements are usually not recognized or supported by college. One ancedotal comment from the director of adult services in an adult degree program at a liberal arts college noted the particular value of a service learning requirement for undergraduates, including adults. This institution discovered the wealth of talent and leadership offered by these adult students through their corporate service commitments as well as their community leadership involvements. These adults provided leadership in enhancing the service outreach of the institution and presented new perspectives on adult students that made an impact on the college community and subsequently the college's standing in the community.

Student Role Responsibilities

The fifth area of influence targets the role and time commitments of being a student. This area is fraught with time and resources issues related to actively pursuing homework and final projects, getting to and from courses and the library, typing papers, collaborating with study groups, and engaging in other activities to support academic success. In addition, most adults need to negotiate and plan time for developing study skills, library information retrieval skills, and computer skills. Research suggests that time management related to college studies continues to be a difficult and ongoing issue for adults. Adults typically suggest that they need far more time for college studies than they can give. They often self-report extensive hours devoted to homework and studying, yet these hours are often "sandwiched in" among work, family activities, and other responsibilities. And often adults express guilt and frustration because they feel they should devote much more time and effort to college studies.

College staff and faculty need to provide helpful information bulletins, short courses, and, when possible, in-class discussions that support adult students in developing time management strategies and study skills; basic computer literacy; and specialized skills for note-taking, test-taking, and library search retrieval strategies. Orientation programs could offer optional information sessions; colleges may also consider offering special one-credit seminars to develop knowledge and skills for student success.

Responsibility to Self

The final and least understood influencer is the role and support of the person—the adult's self. Many adult students report they must sacrifice themselves and their personal needs to meet the needs and demands of their many other responsibilities. Exhaustion, tension, and a diminishing sense of self often lead some adults to drop out of college. College support services can be of value by offering specialized support for being an efficient and effective student. Adults often value the social support of other adult students who can share stories and validate that they are in similar situations and can make it! And some adults find particular value in academic courses that offer self-reflection and exploration, particularly in the humanities or behavioral science areas. These intellectually and emotionally engaging class opportunities offer reappraisals of self and potential validation or growth of life values. Through these experiences, some adults identify a different perspective on what is important and valuable in their lives.

Why be concerned about the self of the adult student, beyond developing information and skills? Many adult students have a wavering self-image and limited self-confidence. Their sense of self will be tested in the collegiate environment, as well as challenged by their external world as they participate in college. Often negative messages, as well as self-doubts, lead to limited energies and productivity in college. Further, initial goals and motives may be weak or unrealistic and may be quickly challenged with participation in a competitive collegiate environment. For some adults, caring faculty and staff provide important reassurances. Other adults, however, self-destruct when faced with challenges and do not follow through on their initial enrollment application or stop out from further college enrollment when difficulties are presented. Staff and faculty need to pay special attention to the self of the adult student and value and support its nourishment.

Understanding the Practitioner's Influence on Adult Participation

What can practitioners do to influence adults to enter college and to persist? Two discussions have proven helpful for both practitioners and researchers alike. Patricia Cross's work (1981) has been particularly influential. Her typology presents primary elements that globally influence the entry of adult students. This perspective also suggests that influencers existing at the beginning of college studies continue to influence adults after they enter. These initial influencers can later become barriers that affect potential stop-out or drop-out behavior. The second discussion presents aggregate adult persister characteristics. This second perspective offers practitioners ways to identify at-risk adult students.

Cross's Typology of Barriers

This typology provides a very helpful framework for understanding the complexity of adult participation and for planning adult-oriented programs, policies, and procedures. Each of these barriers—situational, institutional, dispositional, and informational—help to explain part of the complexity and the dynamics affecting adult lives. The inclusion of informational barriers in this discussion occurred in Darkenwald and Merriam (1982), with further discussion in Merriam and Caffarella (1999). These key barriers also provide a context for understanding the positive and negative valences affecting adult participation:

- **Situational barriers** arise from one's real life situation. They could include financial costs, family conflict, work demands, life traumas, and the balancing of role commitments, as well as other life situational events.
- **Institutional barriers** arise from typical administrative, organizational, and educational practices. These elements include institutional policies towards adult learners; the potential lack of relevant and accessible academic programs and convenient course scheduling; problematic financial supports for students; demeaning faculty or staff; an indifferent academic bureaucracy; or other institutional practices, attitudes, and policies that hinder adult participation.
- **Dispositional barriers** arise from each adult's negative or dysfunctional attitudes and self-perceptions. These elements could include beliefs and actions related to adults' perceptions of themselves as learners, the inability to redefine role and time

commitments, a lack of self-confidence, a belief in perfectionism in one's academic studies, concern about the aging process in relation to pursuing college studies, and other problematic beliefs and values of adult students.

- **Informational barriers** arise from the lack (or overabundance) of information about self, academic possibilities, and programmatic procedures. This area suggests the limited accessibility of helpful and informative information regarding adult-oriented college environments and programs. Lack of knowledge and information resources often becomes a major barrier for adults, both at entry and in their persistence.

Characteristics of Adult Persisters and Nonpersisters

The second approach based on a compilation of descriptive research suggests that adult student persisters and nonpersisters have certain identifiable characteristics (Table 2.1). This approach looks at the comparative differences between early exiting versus graduating adults, suggesting certain probable characteristics of at-risk versus successful adult students. A review of this table may suggest characteristics to emphasize in entry programs, with academic advisement, and for special intervention programs with adult at-risk students. As you examine this table, consider ways in which you and your institution could provide support and specialized resources for at-risk adult students.

INSIDE THE WORLD OF THE ADULT LEARNER

To best recruit and retain adult students, faculty and staff need to gain an insider's understanding of each adult learner's world, which encompasses both the individual's identity as an adult and his or her desire to be a student within a complex web of work, family, student, and community responsibilities. As you continue into Chapter 3, institutional strategies will be presented that also speak to the needs, goals, motives, and life circumstances of adults who desire to be collegiate undergraduate learners.

Table 2.1. Characteristics of Adult Persisters and Nonpersisters

Persisters	Nonpersisters
Parents with college experiences	Parents with high school education level
Past positive experiences in attending college or previous completion of two or more years of college	Past negative college experiences, first time entry into college or limited prior college work
Strong academic abilities	Major deficiencies in basic skills
Clear set of goals and declaration of a concentration (major)	Uncertain goals or unrealistic goals of long-term consequence
Strong study habits and higher aspirations	Difficulty in adjusting to the routines of formal study, insecurity about ability to learn, nervousness about tests, and inadequate work habits
Strong self-discipline and determination	Low-level achievement drives; poor motivation, as well as being indecisive and disorganized
View formal college course work as developing skills in self-directedness	Value formal learning that directly relates to life experiences, often in concrete, practical and specific ways
More often multiplistic or relativistic thinker	Lack of intellectual independence; often a concrete thinker
Support by family, by significant others and by employers	Unclear or negative messages regarding support and valuing of college studies in one's life
Perceived limited family demands	Perceived significant family-work demands
Financial resources from self, family, and work to support college studies	Financial difficulties, both in general and with support of college studies
Flexible in course scheduling and in taking multiple courses	Limited flexibility in scheduling courses and limited time to support course work
Clear support resources from the college and program for adult students	Unclear or limited resources from the college and program to support adult students

(Apps, 1987; Beal & Noel, 1980; Bean & Metzner, 1996; Carter, 1982; Kiger & Johnson, 1997; Knoell, 1976; Malloch & Montgomery, 1996; Naretto, 1995; Spanard, 1990)

CHAPTER 3

Shaping Recruitment, Admission, and Retention: Institutional Responses

We are having decreased enrollments of adult students. Is it the economy? Is it recruiting by entrepreneurial adult degree programs in our market? Is it our environment? What should we be doing differently?—A director of adult program services

I just don't understand it. It looks like we are losing about 30% of our adult students after their first year, their freshman year of enrollment. And it looks like we have lots of adults that don't take a course with us every semester. They enroll maybe one semester and then disappear. What is going on?—A director of nontraditional and reentry student programs

Recruiting and retaining adult students continue to be dominant concerns for both faculty and administrators. How can we best attract adults into our programs? How can we keep our adult learners enrolled, and how can we help them be successful in college? This chapter will focus on institutional strategies and perspectives. Both general and specialized adult marketing and recruitment will be considered. In addition, this chapter will suggest a variety of institutional strategies, policies, and perspectives that could influence the admission and retention of adult students.

HOW DO WE ATTRACT ADULTS TO OUR PROGRAMS?

Each institution and academic program faces several shaping forces as its leaders target an adult audience and construct the type of messages and recruitment campaigns that will attract adult students. Program administrators begin their recruitment efforts by considering their institution's and program's mission and vision for serving adult students. In addition, their efforts must reflect their institution's particular niche in the higher education market and also the particular academic programs, delivery systems, and support services that their institution offers to adult learners.

Recruitment efforts also should consider the demographic and personal characteristics of the desired adult student clientele. Because values, experiences, and emotions shape each adult's search for a college, admissions and marketing must be anchored in understanding the particular adult clientele's beliefs and perspectives, their goals for a college degree, and the world that shapes their access to college. In addition, institutions need to have up-to-date demographic information that characterizes the types of adult students that have been attracted. Such information provides a comparison with desired future growth markets of new adult clientele. By using a demographic tracking system, adult education programs that have existed for 20 years have discovered new clientele and also the shifting perspectives and lifestyle changes influencing that clientele.

General Recruitment and Marketing to Adult Learners

Because most prospective adult students are geographically bounded, residing in the regional community as homeowners and/or jobholders, most adult-oriented programs base their general recruitment efforts on *public communication strategies*. These general marketing strategies draw upon messages that establish institutional reputation and program value to attract particular adult clientele. For example, many adults desire a program tailored to their particular work schedules and to their involvement in demanding work activities; thus, the discussion of access, program features, and related support services through an evening or weekend program would be pivotal. These general public messages are typically communicated to

public venues, including newspaper, television and radio advertisements; home mailer bulletins; highway billboards and bus or
subway posters; community and business education opportunity fairs as well as shopping mall community services displays;
and general newspaper and television press releases and public
service announcements. In addition, adult recruitment could include college or university brochure advertisements, community
agency or organization bulletin advertisements, public kiosks
and movie theater advertisements. One unique recruitment activity was reported by the Cleveland Area College Consortium.
This 11-member consortium targeted local businesses and held
joint college fairs on work sites during employee lunch hours
(Santovec, 1992).

The challenge of directing marketing and recruitment to
the general public involves crafting a message that both captures
adults' attention and also encourages them to seek out information and apply. Because many colleges are competing for that
prospective adult student, public marketing messages must be
unique enough to attract attention and provide name recognition. Most programs recruit by noting adult-oriented program
features that attract adults, such as convenience, access, and
credit for life experience. For example, programs may publicize
the features of evening or weekend program offerings, accelerated degree format or portfolio assessment for life experiences,
or special location and distance learning components.

Many adult students and researchers suggest that adults
pursue college degrees to advance their career, to enhance job
security, and to have greater financial opportunities (Kiger &
Johnson, 1997; Midgen & Bradley, 1992). These motivators can
often be used in crafting recruitment campaigns. Particularly
with community college adult students, job placement rates and
alumni salaries make up important components of the recruitment message. In contrast, adults attending four-year institutions suggest that they often select the institution and program
based on faculty reputation and national rankings of institution
or program, alongside their own interest in career development.
Adults in adult-degree programs particularly value specialized
programs connected to businesses and industries. They also

value the prestige of practitioner instructors and the current work roles of their fellow adult students, and programs that mirror the knowledge and work expectations of their career pursuits. Certain programs specialize in personal and career development, liberal studies, or add-on expertise, such as business management for technical fields; these types of programs offer different messages that speak to the motivations and goals of their targeted clientele.

A growing number of institutions have pursued information technology for recruiting and marketing to adults. These efforts are becoming a common part of recruitment strategy as adults come to recognize and experience access to a significant amount of comparative information through the Web. Unfortunately, many institutions have not created information about their programs that adult learners can easily access. Many Web sites are often hidden by layers of links and broadly focused names that don't alert individuals to adult programs and services. Some beginning resource pages reflect either listings, clearinghouses, or brokering services aimed at adult clientele, similar to the *Peterson's Guide to Colleges*. These efforts often note listings, with limited search functions for the main factors of program, access, and delivery systems. As technology continues to change rapidly, so does adult awareness of its capabilities and uses in finding information.

Examples of varied marketing presentations through the World Wide Web include:

1. Adult-oriented institution, such as
   - Empire State College, http://www.esc.edu/esconline/online1.nsf/esc__hompage
   - Excelsior College [formerly Regents College], *http://www.regents.edu*,
   - Thomas Edison State College *http://www.tesc.edu/*,
   - University of Phoenix *http://www.phoenix.edu/*

2. Divisions or colleges solely directed to adults, such as
   - Heidelberg University—Ohio, Division of Lifelong Learning, *http://www.heidelberg.edu/offices/lifelong*,

- Central Michigan University, College of Extended Learning http://www.cel.cmich.edu/
- University of Maryland University College *http://www. umuc.edu/*

3. Special adult entry discussions into regular collegiate programs, such as
   - University of Louisville, *http://www.louisville.edu/provost/ cont-studies/*,
   - University of Maine System of Distance Education *http://www.learn.maine.edu*,
   - University of Missouri-St. Louis *http://www.umsl.edu/ ~conted/*,
   - University of Oklahoma, College of Continuing Education and College of Liberal Studies *http://tel.occe.ou.edu/*, and

4. Home pages focused upon adult student support services, such as these diverse examples,
   - Arizona State University Office of Student Life, Adult Re-Entry Program *http://www.asu.edu/vpsa/studentlife/ reentry/*,
   - Iowa State University, Off-Campus and Adult Student Services *http://www.ocass.iastate.edu*,
   - Portland State University, Mentor Program for Returning Women Students *http://www.ess.pdx.edu/iasc/rtwspage.htm*,
   - Texas A & M University, Department of Student Life, Adult and Graduate Student Services *http://stulife.tamu. edu/agss/*

Market Differentiated Recruitment

Adult program leaders expend most of their efforts on market differentiated recruitment. These efforts present unique program features designed for a specific adult clientele. Thus, such efforts are often time- and place-sensitive and are presented through media selected to reach particular groups of adults. Given the number of competing program options and the changing circumstances of adults, what does affect recruitment for a targeted set of adult learners? Although the media do influence adults, the personal and organizational environment of the adult program can be equally influential. An adult's initial experience with the institution can be a surprisingly strong influence on the decision to enroll. Strategies for market differentiated recruitment include the following:

Personal Contacts

Word-of-mouth recommendations were the influence most often cited by adult students and leaders of adult degree programs in conversations with the authors. Adults placed significant value on the positive experiences of other adults in their friendship circle who had already been to college. Prospective adult students were particularly influenced by reports of a supportive and flexible adult environment, of quality instruction, and of limited bureaucratic hassles. Personal recommendations were more often influential with adults enrolling in four-year degree programs. Adults in two-year institutions, however, reported knowing fewer adults who were pursuing collegiate degrees and therefore more often made decisions in relation to institutional reputation, location, and cost.

Personal endorsements are often valuable in recruitment efforts. For example, specialized marketing campaigns may use current adult students as recruiters. With additional stipends and sometimes on a volunteer basis, these students serve adult programs by being representatives at community forums and business-site college fairs. Some specialized adult programs ask current students to recommend colleagues or family members who might be interested in further information. A few colleges have recruited and paid current adult students to make personal telephone contacts to prospective adult applicants. These varied forms of adult student contact have proven to be very persuasive in discussing the program and the adult student experience with potential students. Adult students communicate in an authentic way the probability of success and the potential congruence of the program philosophy, teaching style, and curricula with adult student lifestyles and experiences. As another strategy, many marketing campaigns also use adult students' personal stories of success to highlight a program's positive impact upon the learner. Some newspaper or brochure advertisements feature adult student alumni, their current work titles and employers, and sometimes personal statements regarding the program's value.

Targeting Reentry Students

Many program marketers have found that their largest market of prospective students consists of reentry students. Thus, a second key strategy recruits former college students who were dropouts or stopouts. Whether efforts concentrate upon recruiting students to a specialized degree-completion program or providing services that help reentry students to reenroll, adult program leaders recognize that these adults have specialized needs and concerns. No national statistics have been published regarding adult enrollment related to past college backgrounds. Nevertheless, four-year colleges have reported in select research that 60% to 90% of adult student enrollees are reentry. Likewise, two-year colleges have reported that anywhere from 30% to 70% of their adult student enrollees are reentry adult students (Kasworm, 1990). In fact, national four-year college dropout and stopout rates suggest that approximately 60% of undergraduate students do not complete a four-year degree program within a five-year period and often exit college within that five-year period (Tinto, 1987).

Many adult-oriented programs target prospective reentry adult students, recognizing that they come with new motivation and commitment. These students also come with special needs for entry assistance. They often bring a variety of college transcripts and related academic learning experiences. In one research study, reentry adults had experienced 1 to 15 previous collegiate institutions, with the norm reflecting 3 previous institutions (Kasworm & Blowers, 1994). Some of these students had specialized educational experiences such as a technical associate's degree, a nonaccredited proprietary school degree, continuing education credits, or distance learning extension credits.

These reentry adults faced special problems with fitting past academic history into current curricula requirements, and many faced both perceived and real concerns for academic success. They pondered how to reenter a culture that they had abandoned, a culture that had given them problems, or a culture that had not previously seemed relevant to their needs and aspirations. Many suspected that the collegiate environment would not support or value their reentry.

Recruitment strategies for these reentry students should emphasize messages regarding convenient access to services and academic programs for adults and specialized advisement, counseling, and related student services offered by the institution. Another potential subject for recruitment messages involves degree-completion programs. Some programs purposefully link with noncredit adult career counseling services; others offer women-in-transition support groups; and yet others provide specialized assistance for dislocated workers, welfare program recipients, or work-site-contracted services. But above all, reentry adults are looking for personal attention, personal assurances of success, and personal assistance for their specific circumstances.

Special Services and Support

A third influence in recruiting adult students involves their special need for support and assistance. Many adults desire a college where faculty and staff will value and respect them through special structures and programs that support their success. Often marketing campaigns can speak to creating a special place for adults, as well as suggest specific programs that reflect this commitment to serving adults. These messages may also describe special academic skills supports, special lounge and phone access, special financial supports, childcare services, cooperative education options, or future employment opportunities. Select institutions may have an established community reputation for this special support and assistance and highlight this reputation with personal stories from graduated students. (Chapter 6 provides specific information about student support services, and Chapter 4 discusses academic advising.)

In previous research, three subgroups noted the significant influence of special services and support for adult learner recruitment and persistence (Kasworm, 1995a). Adults in community colleges reported that they specifically chose the community college because it was committed to providing a second chance for adults. They reported that they valued the perceived institutional messages of helping *all* students to be successful and the availability of remediation services as top attractions. The second subgroup of adults was attracted to adult-degree programs; this group believed that these specialized programs were directly created for adult students and for no-hassle, one-on-one assistance. They believed that customized adult degree programs and related services were personal, convenient, accessible, and supportive. For example, adult students were impressed when their class books were delivered to them at their first class. They also were impressed that they had one full-time adviser throughout their program who could help with academic, administrative, and personal concerns. The third subgroup, adults entering four-year institutions also valued collegiate messages about special services and supports.

Most of these adults recognized that they did not initially choose to attend or were unable to attend college in their young adult years. Colleges with special services for adults suggested that they were "welcome and could succeed" in this competitive environment. These adults often questioned their lack of background preparation and potential difficulties with reading, writing, and mathematics. They also felt "too old," questioning their mental capacities to do college work and their ability to be accepted in a youth-oriented environment. For these adults, the initial availability of advisement and counseling services was paramount. Many of these adults desired preenrollment discussions. Of most significance to adult students, however, were personal interactions with positive, supportive staff and faculty in their initial contacts with the institution, their first-time registration, and their first few classes. For adults seeking entry or reentry, staff and faculty were highly influential because they demonstrated that they cared, were supportive, and would provide assistance.

Within this influence category, a growing orientation toward a corporate model of individual customer service emerges. Although some adult learners may be unsure, unaware, or anxious, and thus need the special support described above, others are sophisticated and savvy adult consumers. Increasing numbers of colleges are reframing their services to accommodate this particular group of adult learners. These individuals have high expectations, seek out their preferred alternatives, make calculated and negotiated decisions, and desire top service and responsiveness. They don't want to "waste their time" talking to a counselor for an hour, and they don't want to be patronized. They want professional, adult-to-adult services with clear directions, answers, and actions. Although colleges dislike thinking of their services within a business framework, this growing cadre of adults consists of demanding customers with very specific expectations for service. They want it their way! Because adults are continually bombarded by sophisticated marketing campaigns directed at their particular needs, they are impressed with colleges that have adapted their traditional recruitment methods to address the knowledgeable adult learner. They expect tailored letters regarding programs, and they expect college contacts who will work with adult students and their particular interests and needs. In addition, they expect clear-cut procedures that create easy transactions through the college's administrative systems.

Specialized Curricula and Delivery Systems

Specialized curricula and program delivery systems are also noted in the top five attractors for adults seeking a college degree. Adults value programs that are convenient and relevant— programs that fit their current lifestyles and commitments. Because many adults are place-bound and time-pressed, they are often attracted to adult degree programs that offer place-accessible and time-enhanced program features. For example, a customized program for adults featuring an accelerated format, convenient commuting location, evening or weekend scheduling, and a predictable course sequence presents an attractive and valued option. For some adults, distance learning formats offer flexibility when they confront unpredictable work schedules, heavy travel commitments, or family demands. And for others, programs that are based upon a group cohort experience with specialized supports for similar kinds of individuals in the cohort (such as workers, reentry women, or dislocated workers) can also be highly attractive. Certain colleges offer an extension site program for adult access, whether it relies on a particular community, workplace setting, military base, or professional group meeting. And with the continuing growth in cadres of adults who can negotiate with their employers to attend college during portions of the day, several colleges are also creating specialized supportive curricula for this group formatted for early morning, noontime, or afternoon classes.

In the last 10 years, a number of programs have also reformatted curricular offerings, specifically designing curricula that build upon past coursework for a training program, a certificate, a two-year degree, or a completed four-year degree. These curricula offer customized programs directed toward adding more expertise and a credential, while acknowledging the current expertise of the adult. For example, a significant number of baccalaureate programs have been designed to serve nurses with diplomas, and programs for adults who desire to enter the K-12 teaching profession as a second career. Many colleges are now incorporating competency-based curriculum models that rely on validated assessment of prior specialized training and business experiences; programmatic modules to meet the remaining competencies, often for a business, communications, or computer-related degree; and sophisticated transcript and skill audits to create the matrix of completed and to-be-completed knowledge and skill areas for a degree program. This approach involves assessing and validating work experiences, past training activities, and past professional organizational involvement for equivalency to academic course credit.

A unique adult degree program features general studies or liberal studies. These programs offer support for maximum use of past course work while also providing a flexible, interdisciplinary, and often accelerated option toward a bachelor's degree. For adult workers, liberal studies programs provide important integrative thinking, broad interdisciplinary perspectives, and advanced critical analysis skills, rather than a more narrow, skills-oriented degree program.

INSTITUTIONAL STRATEGIES FOR EFFECTIVE ADMISSIONS AND ENTRY

Beyond attractors that institutions can use to recruit adults into the collegiate environment, there are a variety of institutional strategies that also are fundamental influencers for adult admission to college and to their commitment to participate. Anecdotal evidence suggests that of the pool of adults who make initial contact regarding admissions, only one of five students enter into a freshmen experience, and only one of three reenter the collegiate environment after a break in enrollment. Thus, institutional strategies beyond recruitment and marketing are the second important support base to influence adult enrollment.

Policies and Procedures for Admissions and Initial Registration

Policies and procedures that shape the admissions, orientation, and initial course registration process become prominent influences on adults as they enter college. As the previous discussions indicate, adults are attracted to programs that understand their current life circumstances and provide supportive entry through people, programs, and recruitment strategies. Many leaders of adult-oriented programs have reassessed their admissions policies based on their analysis of factors that predict adult student academic success at their institutions. For example, a growing number of institutions have modified admissions policies for individuals who are 25 years of age or older or who have had a five-year break between school participation and their current admissions. For example, Kasworm and Pike (1994) found that neither SAT nor ACT scores, nor past high school grades, for adults of 30 years of age or older predicted academic success.

Many colleges have established special admissions criteria for adult students, which may include alternative assessment mechanisms such as reviews of current work vita, statements of goals for college enrollment, writing samples, or basic skills tests. Some colleges have a two-stage admissions process, placing adults with potential academic difficulties into an entry probationary admission status and required adult-learner-based courses. Successful performance moves them into admitted student status. Some colleges have a required diagnostic and orientation workshop for select adults to provide them with special skills, information, and support, as well as to evaluate their abilities to perform in their academic environment.

Evaluating Prior Academic Credit

In the admissions and enrollment process, adults often have major concerns about transferring past credit and the congruence of past collegiate work to meet current institutional credit requirements. Supportive institutions have created strategies to efficiently evaluate past course work and alternative program curriculum guides to aid adults. These strategies include specialized individual advisement and review of transcripts in the early stages of the admissions and registration processes, often using degree audit software. Because of the diversity of prior institutional involvement, however, staff often must provide specialized review in transcript assessment. Be forewarned: many adults will avoid institutions that will not or cannot evaluate transcripts until the middle of their first semester of enrollment.

Academic Forgiveness Policies

Upon admission and successful academic involvement, many institutions have policies for academic forgiveness (sometimes called second opportunity or academic bankruptcy policies). Adult students find this particular policy to be psychologically uplifting. Some adults have suggested that it was a decisive factor in their sticking it out in college. The policy is directed to adults who have reentered and performed well in their recent courses. However, their transcript presents a history of past C's, D's, and F's. The policy provides a petition process and sometimes a hearing for adults who request that their earlier course work not be included in their current GPA. Thus, these learners gain a second chance to prove they can be currently successful in their academic role. For many adult students who were unfocused and produced lackluster grades in their young adult college years, this policy has often created a special confidence and motivation for them to be successful and academically energized. As an example, note excerpts from the Academic Second Opportunity policy at the University of Tennessee—Knoxville (Academic Policies and Regulations, 2000), which is part of the university's undergraduate retention standards:

> The Academic Second Opportunity is designed to assist the student who was not successful in progressing toward a degree during a previous attendance at UT but is now performing satisfactory work. . . . An undergraduate student may petition for Academic Second Opportunity upon meeting the following requirements: 1) the student has re-enrolled following an absence from UT of at least three full calendar years; 2) the student's previous academic record at the University was unsatisfactory (normally, below a C average); 3) since readmission, the student has completed 15 or more graded hours (correspondence coursework may not be included in the 15 hours), earning a 2.5 GPA or above. . . . Decisions on granting Academic Second Opportunity are made by committee. If the student's petition is approved, all previous academic work will remain on the permanent record, but the grades for such work will not be used in computing the gradepoint average or in determining academic standing. Previous credits earned with a grade of C or better will continue to meet major, distribution, and graduation requirements. To graduate, a student granted Academic Second Opportunity must complete at least 30 hours at UT following readmission.

Assessment of Prior Knowledge

Many adults value and seek out institutions that offer either portfolio assessment or alternative testing to evaluate prior knowledge competencies. Initial admissions and entry policies need to provide clear and complete discussions of these processes and how they fit into curricular structures. Although portfolio assessment and alternative assessments of prior knowledge are very attractive to adult applicants, many adults decide upon matriculation that the self-directed assessment efforts demand too much time and energy. For example, one administrator of an adult-centered institution noted that approximately one-third of the institution's adult enrollees stated they selected the institution based in part on the opportunity to use the portfolio assessment option; nevertheless, only about 20% of that group actually pursued those alternatives (Anonymous conversations, 1995).

In one study of both two- and four-year institutions with adult degree policies and procedures, data revealed that 79% of the institutions offer the College Level Examination Program, with slightly fewer (74%) offering Advanced Placement Exams (Flint, 1999). Over half of the institutions offered both local challenge or proficiency exams. About one-third used noncollegiate sponsored education guides, College Credit Recommendation Service, and about the same percentage were involved with the American College Testing Proficiency Examination Program (Kasworm, 1995b; Flint, 1999). For additional information, program leaders may wish to consult with a leading organization for alternative assessment, the Council for Adult and Experiential Learning (CAEL). Its Web site at http://www.cael.org/ offers further information on prior learning assessment (PLA).

Entry Basic Skills Assessment

Depending upon the college and the program, preentry English and math skill tests may be required and may prove valuable in retaining adult students. Based on research findings, most adults view these basic skill assessments as extremely helpful and supportive of their later success. They also believe that these assessments can be invaluable in the advising process for initial course selection.

RETENTION STRATEGIES

Helping adults to stay enrolled and to succeed with degree completion are important goals. No simple set of interventions exists, however, that will "keep" adults in college. For example, several studies have found that adult women students with young children are more likely to drop out, whereas other studies have shown that adult students with children are more persistent than adult students without dependent children. Clearly, each individual's situation should be valued and understood in its complexity by considering the diverse factors that can support or hinder continued enrollment. Practitioners need to recognize that adults lead negotiated lives across many roles and responsibilities. It is evident that multiple factors interact that potentially can contribute to withdrawal from college; often adults will suggest socially acceptable reasons for their actions rather than reveal the true complexity of their concerns.

Those who lead and administer adult-oriented program efforts must continue to research, innovate for, and listen to adult students. The loss of enrolled adult students is a highly costly one for both the institution and the individual student. One study based on exit surveys of adult students who had withdrawn suggested that 31% planned to return and resume work on their degrees within a 12-month period. Of those, less than 13% actually did reenroll within a 30-month period (Wright & Spanard, 1988). Thus, this study suggested that 87% of adults who leave an institution do not return in a two-and-a-half year period. One critic suggested that the untold story in these statistics is the choice of adult students to attend another institution to meet their goals, rather than return to his or her past college situation. Many adult programs have attempted to compare their attrition rates with others and have found that there are no helpful comparative statistics. This frustration comes, in part, because each adult program pinpoints a highly specific grouping of adults, within a specific context. And adult students are mobile and do have choices. Thus, some adult programs are collaborating to develop benchmarking data and statistical comparisons across similar types of programs in parallel geographic and educational environments.

Adult-oriented program leaders recognize that they enter into a *partnership* with each adult student. Their first responsibility for retaining adult students is to provide the best adult-oriented environment. Second, they need to find ways to enhance adults' psychological support systems for entry and for continuance. Third, programs can provide supporting linkages with each adult's key environments. Attending college does involve each student's other spheres of influence; thus, college should consider support activities for spouse and children, work site or employer-related support activities, and occasionally community-related support activities. Last, program leaders recognize that adult success and retention come from shaping innovative programs, delivery systems, and instructional environments reflecting the adult learner.

Ten Institutional Retention Strategies

Throughout this book, many broad and specific strategies that influence retention are described. The following list provides a brief overview of 10 primary strategies. These actions and strategies can be reviewed in detail throughout this book to determine their fit with your institution, its academic programs for adults, and the particular types of adults attracted to your environment.

1. Initial entry advisement, orientation, and career counseling are pivotal activities for adult retention. Most adults are entering into a unique culture that is often assumed to be youth oriented and to value intellectually gifted young adults. They may feel somewhat alienated and experience challenges, questions, and amazement at this environment. Most don't have a clear understanding or background regarding the important actions, language, and processes of college registration and curricula involvement. For support and success, adults need early systems of orientation, advisement, and support by sensitive and knowledgeable staff and faculty. Two valuable resources for practitioners about providing adult transitions into college are Steltenpohl and Shipton's (1986) article and Schlossberg, Lynch, and Chickering's book (1989) on creating collegiate environments that matter for adult students.

2. Financial assistance has been shown to be a significant issue for many adult students in their initial decision to enter;

more often than not it is the key issue for continuing college. Many adult programs have created special workshops to aid adult students with strategies for using existing resources and finding additional assistance. Of greatest impact, many programs have identified resource people in the financial aid office who can provide adult students with assistance regarding various financial options, including work study, loans, and other resources that relate to their adult circumstances. A growing number of colleges and adult programs have developed special adult scholarship programs, sometimes with local professional groups or businesses that support adult student involvement in higher education. For example, Iowa State University has a scholarship program for adult students and the Ada Comstock program at Smith College offers a special full scholarship to a select group of adult women. One innovative institutional strategy reflects a "rainy day" fund— emergency loans for students, often to help them with initial registration costs or book costs, as well as family emergencies that could cause them to drop out.

   3. Academic and basic skills development has been a "hidden" issue for both adult and younger students. Adult-oriented program leaders need to work creatively with current institutional resources by integrating short seminars, a first-year experience semester-long course, orientation programs, special courses to improve cognitive and study strategies, as well as courses for providing remediation in reading, writing, and mathematics. One unique strategy discovered in the Kasworm and Blowers's study was that some adult students self-identified their needs and enrolled in a community college to strengthen their skills before they reentered a four-year college. If you are concerned about this issue, look to Grosset's 1991 study reporting that the most important factor in the persistence of adult students was a positive self-assessment of study skills and perceived readiness for academic demands.

   4. Adult-oriented policies and procedures are another major source of concern for current adult students. Many policies create special stress, as well as logistical and personal problems for adult students. Adults desire collegiate personnel and an environment that recognizes they are responsible adults who often work 8 to 5 in another place distant from the campus and who need ways to conduct business that are convenient and accessible. Adults desire an environment and a system that supports and embraces the adult learner. The list of possible adult-sensitive policies, procedures, and programs covers a large territory of possibilities. One helpful resource for practitioners is the American Council of Education guide entitled *Focus on Adults—A Self-Study Guide for Postsecondary Education Institutions* (2001).

5. **Information technology** can provide another source of potential support for adult students. An increasing number of adult-oriented programs are experimenting with listservs, threaded classroom conversations, and other forms of information technology to provide additional service and support for adult students. Although some of these efforts are obviously in an experimental stage, certain groups of adults—particularly those already engaged in technological activities through their work—find connection with their classmates, faculty, and the college via computing technology to be extremely helpful. In addition, these adult students have found value in creating a cyber learning community and in being able to gain access to support services personnel and to resolve many institutional concerns without coming onto campus. Although distance learning formats can be highly accessible and seductive for time-starved adults, these formats may reflect problems such as the lack of appropriate adult learning designs and adult student support. Rumors and select institutional research suggest that the dropout rate for adults in distance learning courses ranges between 30% to 70% exiting prior to end of course.

6. **Programs that incorporate families and spouses** matter because these significant others are usually supporters who reinforce the collegiate experience. In fact, several studies suggest that adult student persistence is directly connected with the positive support of family and spouse. Adult-oriented programs can provide an important support base by incorporating family and spouse through special orientation sessions, open houses, and family recreation or cultural gatherings. Adult students suggest that college should become a family affair, rather than exclusively focused on single young adults' social needs.

7. Personal interaction with and attention from staff and faculty is a very important source of support for adult student persistence. Each faculty and staff member should make the best of each contact, because it may be the only contact. Adult students do vote with their feet. If they find a hostile environment, they leave when they can identify a better alternative.

8. Special needs services, such as housing, transportation, security, and childcare, become important considerations in adult persistence. Leaders of colleges and universities who want their programs to serve adults must continue to consider diverse segments of the adult population, adult needs, and effective ways to serve adults through campus and community resources.

9. Adult support networks on some campuses have proven to be invaluable. Examples at the University of Wyoming, Texas A & M University, and many other colleges and universities demonstrate that adult student groups can exert a very powerful and positive force for a select group of students. Some campuses have used adult student peer mentors for entering adults. And a number of institutions have special adult professional organizations and adult honor societies recognizing adult academic achievements. As with the other retention strategies, however, this strategy is important for one subset of adults—those who value friendship and connectedness with others at college. Although many adults consider peer social activities to be a luxury they can live without, for others its makes the college their place of comfort and friendship.

10. Knowledge of each adult student is the obvious retention strategy. Retention strategies should have this knowledge as their foundation. Ideally the adult student should be individually known and have ongoing interactions with specific collegiate personnel. Any strategy should draw upon this knowledge of the adult, whether it is proactive services, academic programs and policies, or the broader concerns of faculty and staff for an adult-friendly environment. Each institution and program should create appropriate efforts that represent its particular adult students, the culture in which these adults interact, and the resources that best serve adults as partners in the collegiate learning experience.

IDENTIFYING THE BEST SET OF SOLUTIONS

Recruiting and retaining students is the responsibility of everyone in the college. This chapter suggests that you need to consider both general and differentiated marketing strategies, as well as the complex set of institutional policies, programs, activities, and services that both attract entry and offer support for retention. In the next chapter, Chapter 4, one other part of this solution set is discussed—the importance of academic advisement and, in particular, developmental counseling to provide the ongoing support for the changing needs and concerns of the adult learner.

CHAPTER 4

Providing a Road Map:
Academic Advisement

Deadlines and due dates are more difficult for persons with a family than single students. More consideration of adults with families and work schedules would help ease some stress. Also, advisors who are well informed, considerate, and have your future in mind would help. I hate being treated like an inexperienced youngster who does not know what they want or what their goals are.—34-year-old student

Most advisors believe that since we are older, we do not need the guidance that an 18-year-old entering freshman needs. This is wrong. I spent 20 years in the Army, around the world. But I do not (or did not) know any more about university procedures and life than did any other freshman. Forget my age and treat me like any other student. I may be 40, but I am not a peer of faculty and staff.—40-year-old student

These quotes illustrate the complexity surrounding academic advising and adult learners. What may be viewed as alienating to one adult student can be seen as absolutely critical to the next. Some adult learners enter with clear-cut academic goals, feeling confident in their ability to negotiate the collegiate environment, only to feel marginalized when advisors treat them as a traditional students. Others express a strong desire for advisors who are prepared to help them navigate this new environment. This chapter will address the various challenges that adults enounter throughout their college attendance. The advising process will also be discussed, and an action agenda for advisors will be presented.

As discussed earlier, adult learners possess characteristics that are both similar and dissimilar to the traditional-age college student. They may experience different academic, vocational, and personal concerns than many of their younger counterparts. Nevertheless, they also may expect many of the same things out of the advising relationship that traditional-aged students want—advisors who are accessible, up-to-date, and informed.

All students need strong support services to help them be successful and achieve their goals in college. Academic advising is perhaps the most critical of these services. It is the one vehicle that ensures students will interact with a concerned institutional representative. Advisors may be the *only* exchange the adult student has with the institution that directly deals with his or her individual needs. Because many adults either commute to campus or are based off campus, the advisor is often their only out-of-class contact with the institution.

Although students may be assigned a formal advisor, student affairs professionals often assume informal advising roles. Environments that foster the attitude that advising involves a responsibility shared among faculty, administrators, and student affairs and advising offices or centers will increase the likelihood of retaining adult learners.

A variety of institutional models for delivering academic advising exist. These models have shifted dramatically from systems in which faculty alone provided advising to the point where currently less than half of today's campuses rely on faculty to carry out this responsibility (Habley, 2000). Today, more than ever before, campuses are more likely to offer specialized advising services to special student populations, including adult learners. To expect that all institutions, however, will be able to provide specialized services geared to the unique needs of diverse segments of their student populations places unrealistic demands on institutions. For advisors to prepare for and address such needs, developmental academic advising becomes imperative.

Advising based on the premise that the advisor is responsible for facilitating student growth and success is referred to as "developmental academic advising." Crockett offers the following definition of developmental advising:

Academic advising is a developmental process which assists students in the clarification of their life and career goals and in the development of career plans for the realization of these goals. It is a decision-making process by which students realize their maximum educational potential through communication and information exchanges with an advisor; it is continuous, multifaceted and the responsibility of both the student and the advisor. The advisor serves as a facilitator of communication, a coordinator of learning experiences through course and career planning and academic progress review, and an agent of referral to other campus agencies as necessary. (1984, p.1)

Developmental advising advocates a shared responsibility between advisor and the student. It promotes initiative and growth in students and can lead to enriched academic experiences. A central feature of developmental advising is that it reflects a continuous process. What adult learners will need from their advisors will be determined by where they are in their degree programs.

ACADEMIC ADVISING AS
A CONTINUOUS PROCESS

Effective academic advisement involves more than merely registering students for classes. The following section describes what academic advisors can do to assist adult learners not only as they begin their higher education experience, but also as they move through and out of the system.

Becoming a Student

Adult learners require different institutional responses based on whether they are moving into, through, or out of higher education (Schlossberg, Lynch, & Chickering, 1989). When adults begin their higher education experiences, they confront a different set of rules, regulations, norms, and expectations. Advisors play a critical role in helping adults during this adjustment process. Identifying each adult learner's motivations for entering or, in many cases, returning to college is an important place to begin the advising process.

An earlier chapter noted that adults frequently come to college in response to some life transition. By encouraging advisees to discuss their transitions and the factors that motivated them to enroll, advisors can help students determine if their return was a snap decision in response to a crisis, or one that was well-considered.

Exploring Issues Related to College Attendance

To explore the type of transition the advisee is encountering, advisors can ask learners how they view their return to college—is it at a good time or a bad time? Is it something they are excited about, or is it something they feel is being thrust upon them? Sometimes adults in transition become immobilized and fail to see options. When appropriate, advisors should help these students consider all options available to them, whether or not they include a return to school.

The transition into college adds to the stress of existing transitions. During the initial advising meeting, advisees should be encouraged to discuss how their personal and situational constraints will affect their transition to college. Are they coming back to school with the full support of family members and co-workers? What other commitments do they have outside the classroom that might compete for their time? These kinds of information help advisors understand the type and degree of support each learner may need.

Of equal importance is asking advisees to reflect on their preparations for the changes created by their transition to school. Advisors can help advisees consider potential liabilities such as strained family and personal relationships, increased financial concerns, and concurrent commitments and stress. This reality check should be balanced by discussing the strengths the adult learner brings to college (for example, knowledge of the world of work and experience) as well as strategies that might help the student counteract existing liabilities.

Juggling the Student Role

Most adult learners consistently juggle the demands of adulthood (including parenting, full-time employment, and elder care) in addition to college attendance. Their success in college can be influenced by advisors who encourage them to realistically assess existing loads. These loads can be external, involving family, work and community responsibilities. Or they can be internal, related to their personal aspirations, desires, and expectations for themselves as learners. Critical to the advising process is determining each learner's power to cope with these load demands.

Advisors can help advisees determine their power to cope with these loads by encouraging them to examine their external resources (such as family support and economic status) and their internal resources (their acquired skills, coping ability, and personality). Carefully examining these two factors helps to determine the "margin" that each student has available for dealing with the demands required by the student role.

The usefulness of examining a learner's margin was initially suggested by McClusky (1970). Basic components of his "theory of margin" as they apply to advising adults in higher education are as follows: (a) learning situations require expenditures of resources (time, energy, money); (b) each advisee has a limited supply of resources, and the amount available to each advisee will vary; (c) advisees have various responsibilities (as spouses, parents, and employees) that account for the load they must balance in conjunction with their student role; (d) resources such as financial and family support make an impact on each advisee's power; and (e) margin is the amount of power the advisee has available over and beyond that required to handle her or his existing load.

Margin can be increased by reducing the load or increasing power, or it can be decreased by increasing the load, reducing power, or both. Whenever possible, advisors should help advisees explore strategies for increasing their power (such as becoming less involved in community activities or seeking assistance with childcare). These discussions can help advisees make critical enrollment decisions. For example, advisors who overlook a student's margin when developing course schedules can in fact contribute to assigning a course load that may ultimately end in the student's withdrawal. Discussions of margin must be revisited frequently because a learner's margin can change drastically while learners pursue their degree programs (for example, with the loss of a spouse or a job). It is important for advisors to remember that new advisees may be unprepared and unaware of student role demands and that advisors may need to provide this valuable insight.

Preparing for Role Changes

The transition into a student role involves role changes for adults. The degree of difficulty associated with a role change frequently depends on how well an individual understands the expectations and norms associated with that role. Adult learners often look to their advisors for guidance about what those expectations involve. Advisees with no prior higher education experience may not even know what questions need to be asked, and advisors may have to help formulate them or to anticipate special needs.

In addition to providing up-to-date and accurate information such as course offerings and course sequences, advisors may initially need to address issues related to understanding academic procedures and institutional routines. Answering such trivial questions as where to park, how to purchase textbooks, and how to drop or add a class can do much to alleviate the anxieties associated with role change.

First-time students or those who are returning after a prolonged absence may have limited knowledge of the expectations associated with the student role. Many will be anxious about their ability to perform. Some set exceedingly high standards for themselves but lack a sense of the time commitment required to succeed. Advisors thus become a key source of information about how to determine appropriate course load and the special demands that may be associated with various courses.

Being a Student

Identifying Potential Barriers

Throughout the advising process, it is crucial that advisors assess the barriers adult students might confront as they enter and continue through college. As discussed in Chapter 2, researchers (Cross, 1981; Darkenwald & Merriam, 1982) have categorized potential barriers into four areas: situational, institutional, informational, and dispositional. Advisors need to be aware of these barriers and their impact on students and, when feasible, to help eliminate or reduce that impact.

Situational barriers stem from each learner's life situation. Although academic advisors frequently cannot eliminate the situational barriers that adults bring to the learning environment (note Chapter 2), they can be sensitive to how these issues might affect each learner's chances for success. An examination of situational barriers can be useful in determining such things as course load and needed campus resources. For example, if an advisor determines that an adult student may have some financial constraints, it might be wiser to advise the learner to take fewer courses and thus lower tuition-related expenses than to advise the learner to enroll full-time, which might lead to their ultimate withdrawal.

Advisors are frequently called upon to intercede when adult students encounter institutional barriers. These barriers arise from typical administrative, organizational, and educational practices. Many institutions, despite increasing adult student enrollments, have maintained policies, procedures, forms, and other administrative operations created for a traditional-age student population. These are often inappropriate for adult learners (for example, requiring ACT or SAT scores for admissions, parental consent forms, or parents' salary information for financial aid). Advisors must advocate developing appropriate processes to be used with this population if institutional barriers are to be eliminated for the adult learner. In some instances, the advisor must assist the institution in distinguishing between conventional and real policy requirements. Such distinctions can be critical to overcoming institutional barriers confronted by adults.

Because of their off-campus responsibilities, adult learners may encounter informational barriers. These barriers may be present when learners lack information about routines, policies, and program options. Advisors may find the channels of communication that are traditionally used ineffective in advising adult learners. For example, relying on the college newspaper to relay important deadlines and procedures may be ineffective with the off-campus student. To avoid creating informational barriers for adult learners, identifying alternative communication vehicles, such as e-mail and home mailings is critical.

Dispositional barriers arise from each adult's attitudes and self-perceptions. Such barriers could include beliefs and actions related to the learner. Adult advisees may bring memories of past educational endeavors that haunt them in their current efforts to succeed in higher education. Frequently these experiences have eroded their self-confidence. They may be embarrassed by their previous performance, and also anxious over their ability to do college work. Some may express a fear of failure compounded by the fact that they may feel "too old to learn." Dispositional barriers seldom disappear quickly, and advisors must be alert to how these barriers can contribute to the stress advisees experience throughout their college experiences. The need for continued advisor support and understanding may be of paramount importance to these learners.

Exploring Issues of Support

Advisors of adults must often address advising concerns that they may not have encountered with traditional-age students. For example, adult advisees may need guidance in how to negotiate with families, employers, coworkers, and friends to establish priorities, time commitments, and responsibilities. Rather than receiving support and understanding as they undertake a new role, these students may encounter the increased stress of needing to justify to others their decision to enroll. If the external resistance they encounter is not balanced with institutional support, advisees may conclude that their participation is not worth the struggle.

Adults enter higher education with varying levels of support from family members, friends, coworkers, and their communities. Although there are limitations to the amount of support and assistance that can be provided by those not directly involved in the academic environment, assessing the type of external support or stress can be helpful. Determining who their "cheerleaders" are (individuals who are pulling for them, encouraging them to return to college) and who their "toxics" are (individuals likely to sabotage their efforts to get their degree) will help the advisor assess the type of support each learner needs.

Many adult students will need to find new avenues for support. Advisors can encourage such students to widen their support base by connecting them with other adult learners. Research has confirmed that peer networks can contribute to adult student retention (Vanderpool & Brown, 1994). Advisors may want to initiate efforts to establish a peer telephone network. Not only can peer leaders provide important insights into campus life and institutional resources to entering adult learners, they also can provide important sources of assistance. An important by-product of peer networks is the ability to identify high risk adult learners (those most likely to drop out). Advisors may want to ask peer leaders to provide a telephone log of their contacts, noting learners who have volunteered information regarding difficulty in classes, problems with juggling multiple roles, and demands from other stressors that could affect the learner's ability to succeed. This would alert advisors to potential high-risk learners who could benefit from an advisor contact. It is important to note that students involved in peer networks should receive training and should not be seen as advisor replacements. Vanderpool and Brown (1994) provide useful suggestions for initiating peer networks that advisors can use to identify students who may require a more intrusive form of academic advising.

Providing Intrusive Advising

Adult advisees may be hesitant to seek help, often believing they should be able to handle the problem themselves. When they do seek help, it is often too late. This situation becomes further complicated by adult learners' off-campus lives, which often leave them unconnected to resources that could help them attain necessary survival skills. For these reasons, adult student advisors may at times need to be more intrusive than they previously have been.

To troubleshoot for potential high-risk advisees, advisors should monitor students' progress throughout the year, not just at registration time. For example, after the first three weeks of the term, advisors can initiate contact with advisees via a post card listing office hours, an e-mail address, a telephone number, and an invitation to contact them if advisees need assistance or just want to let the advisor know how they are doing. Although not all advisees will respond, such an invitation may make a critical difference in whether or not a student feels encouraged to ask for help. A variation would be to send a departmental newsletter that includes information about the typical concerns of adult students as well as available academic support services.

Intrusive advising has been associated with high retention rates. Students who appear to be high risk should also be contacted after six weeks. By this time, many will have had a major examination or project grade and, on that basis, be more ready to seek assistance.

Advisors can use mid-term grades as a basis for encouraging advisees to examine the likelihood of completing their courses successfully. In some cases, students may need assistance with dropping a course. Others may need assistance in preparing better for the remaining portion of the course. For example, issues related to rusty study skills may not become apparent until the student is confronted with his or her first test. Referrals to study skills courses or individual tutoring may be appropriate. In some cases, encouraging a learner to participate in test-taking seminars and writing, reading, and math refresher courses will be helpful, as will information about seminars on time and stress management.

A central component of intrusive advising for adults may be identifying and connecting them to a full range of campus and community resources. Appropriate referrals to other trusted sources who are good at working with adults can be critical to retaining this student population.

Leaving the Student Role

As adult learners begin to transition from the undergraduate collegiate environment, their need for advising will persist. For many, issues surrounding employment will be the central concern. Whereas some adults continue employment in organizations where they have been employed throughout college, others will seek careers in new areas and will need assistance in understanding the career search process. Career placement services are usually responsible for assisting these advisees in locating new jobs, writing resumes, or learning interviewing techniques. Advisors can supplement these efforts by connecting advisees with previous program graduates and using professional networks to help learners identify potential job openings.

Some advisees may choose to explore the possibility of attending graduate school. Information about graduate school admission requirements, how to prepare for the Graduate Record Examination, how to identify quality graduate degree programs, and how to apply for graduate assistantships are a few things with which advisors are expected to help. Writing letters of recommendation and referring students to specific graduate faculty members may be other ways in which undergraduate advisors can assist their advisees.

No uniformity exists in what adult learners may need during the moving-on stage. For many, this stage requires learners to leave behind what has become a familiar institution and comfortable routines. Some have become dependent on the intellectual stimulation college attendance provides, and most have established routines that must be readjusted. Friendships that have offered support and interpersonal satisfaction will be difficult to maintain, which may produce anxiety.

Many advisors and institutions may not be aware of how important it is to support advisees as they leave the collegiate environment. Schlossberg, Lynch, and Chickering (1989) suggested that advisors can help adults bring closure to their college experience by conducting oral interviews. They recommend including interview questions designed to help adults integrate their knowledge: Has your degree program met your expectations? Did you discover your goals changed as you progressed through your degree? What would you identify as your most significant learning? Other questions might ask learners to focus on the future: What goals do you have for the next five or ten years? How do you envision your life changing in work, home, and leisure? What role will learning have in your further development? And other questions might solicit suggestions on ways to improve the program.

Whether moving in, through, or out of higher education, adult advisees need access to an academic advisor. Students who are also full-time employees will find it difficult to use advising services during traditional office hours. To adequately serve this population, advising times should be extended into evening and weekend hours. Serving advisees who are enrolled in off-campus programs will require the advisor to seek alternative ways to communicate: the telephone, e-mail, and advisor-created Web pages can be helpful to such adults (Polson, 2000). Each advisor will need to decide which advising format provides the most effective continuous access.

To summarize, academic advising should be oriented toward providing information, removing barriers, presenting options, facilitating decision making, and making connections with needed resources. Advisors play a critical role in helping adult students to understand, develop, and make full use of their potential strengths. They are also critical because they work to minimize the negative impact of the transitions revolving around college attendance.

To provide effective academic advising, advisors must recognize that the advising needs of adult students reflect their unique circumstances and that these needs shift as students move through the undergraduate experience. In addition to knowing the institution and its academic processes and staying aware of potential referral resources, advisors must be sensitive to individual differences, and they must be flexible in dealing with unique circumstances. Keeping these requirements in mind, one's understanding of the advising process can be furthered by following a structured model.

THE ACADEMIC ADVISING PROCESS: AN ACTION AGENDA

In 1972, O'Banion introduced the first model of academic advising. Included in his model were five dimensions that can be used to guide the academic advising process. In addition, the model emphasizes the sequential development of an academic program and advising relationship. It suggests a team approach to include professional counselors or academic advisors, peer advisors, and faculty advisors. Emphasis is placed on each individual student's responsibility for decision making. The steps integral to this model include the following: (a) exploring life goals, (b) exploring career goals, (c) choosing a program, (d) choosing courses, and (e) scheduling courses. Although the model was created with the traditional-age student in mind, with certain adaptations, it can be useful in advising adult learners.

Step 1. Exploring Life Goals

To effectively assist learners in exploring life goals, advisors should be aware of student characteristics and development, understand the decision-making process, and have skills in interviewing or counseling. Given that advisors come from different disciplines with different sets of skills, many will be more uncomfortable in assisting advisees in this exploration stage than others will. The book *Counseling Adults in Transition: Linking*

Practice With Theory (Schlossberg, Waters, & Goodman, 1995) is a recommended resource for those who feel less confident in these areas.

Traditional age students enter college dealing with the transition from late adolescence to young adulthood. They have a commonality of age and of developmental issues. Many are just beginning to examine life goals realistically. In contrast, adult students represent a variety of developmental stages and phases. Any number of developmental variables could influence an adult's degree pursuit. For this reason, it is crucial to understand adult development theories. These will sensitize advisors to the many life challenges and issues their advisees may be confronting.

Unlike their younger counterparts who may be discovering who they are, adult learners are often reformulating and refining their identity; and higher education plays an important part in the process. For many, the student role serves as a bridge from one identity to a new one (Breese & O'Toole, 1994). Although most advisors are not trained counselors, they can be effective in assisting advisees to explore life goals and to relate these to degree programs. Advisors might ask questions such as the following:

Questions To Encourage Advisees To Explore Life Goals

1. What are some of the goals you have set for yourself, or what do you see yourself doing with your life in the next 10 or 20 years?

2. Are these goals different from those you used to have? If yes, in what way?

3. What kinds of things are most important to you in your life?

4. How was your decision to seek your degree related to your life goals?

5. Are you enrolling as a result of some big change in your life?

6. How do you think your transition to school will alter your life? How prepared do you feel for the changes this transition will create?

7. In what ways do you think your previous roles and experiences will help you in school?

8. Are you active in the community? In what way?

9. What kinds of friends do you like to have?

10. What are your favorite leisure activities?

Step 2. Exploring Career Goals

Adults may be seeking a college degree for the first time; others are reentering to complete programs initiated earlier. Like traditional college students, many older students are concerned about their careers, but their reasons may be more diverse. While some adults are preparing for their first career, others are initiating a midlife career change. Some are making voluntary career changes, while others are undertaking a career change involuntarily. Some are seeking opportunities to acquire new skills and knowledge that will enhance their career prospects. Whatever the motivation, it has been found that adult students commonly lack confidence in their career decision-making abilities; most welcome advisor assistance.

Understanding the changing nature of work in society and having a broad knowledge of opportunities are important assets for advisors who work with students at this exploration stage. Equally important is knowledge of how to interpret vocational tests or knowledge of resource people who can administer and interpret these tools.

It is at this stage that advisors should ask adult advisees to discuss their preenrollment career aspirations. In doing so, they may find that the learner needs to be encouraged to explore alternative career options. Original career choices may have been established using outdated assumptions about the workforce. This discussion can be particularly important to initiate with returning adults who reenroll in the degree programs previously pursued. Although many may be realistically committed to their original goals, career fields often change in important ways. Many learners lack a clear understanding of the labor market trends and may need to be encouraged to examine these trends in relation to their career choices. And many new career options may exist that returning learners have not explored.

Advisors can also play an important part in helping adults to evaluate how previous career and life decisions have affected the viability of current goals. Many adult learners have made their initial career decisions based solely on personal needs and preferences. But now these adults need to consider family members and current job commitments as they plan their future careers. Such commitments may affect career mobility, and therefore degree options, because of geographic constraints.

Adult advisees may need assistance in labeling existing skills that could be transferred to alternative career options. Locating career options that capitalize on these assets (such as problem-solving abilities) while recognizing existing liabilities (such as health problems) is also important. In some instances, the advisor may need to refer students to campus resource people who are better qualified to assist in this process. The following questions, however, would be useful in initial discussions:

Questions To Encourage Advisees To Explore Career Goals

1. If you could chose any career in the world, what might it be?

2. As far back as you can remember, what are some of the general occupational fields you have considered?

3. What fields have you been thinking about recently?

4. Five years from now, what kind of work environment would you like?

5. Thinking about any previous jobs you may have held, what aspects did you like about them? Dislike? Why?

6. What do you think are your best personal qualities?

7. How strong do you assess your decision-making skills to be?

8. What do you see as your strengths in doing college work?

9. What do you see as your limitations?

10. What do your friends like most about you?

Step 3. Exploring Program Choices

Advisors involved at Step 3 will need to know what programs are available in the institution, program requirements (such as special time commitments, entrance requirements, and fees), and the kinds of outcomes achieved by students who have undertaken those programs.

Many people assume that adult learners enroll with clearer educational goals than traditional-age students. This is not necessarily true. Adult learners often come with short-term goals related to the issues they are confronting, and these issues sometimes cloud the discovery of long-term goals. Advisors need to help students differentiate between short-term goals that are related to long-term aspirations and those that distract students from dealing with the "big picture."

Adults frequently have little flexibility in when and where they take coursework. During this stage of the process, advisors need to assist learners in identifying what degree programs can be completed within the learner's time and location constraints. If a program cannot be completed within these constraints, it cannot be considered a viable option, no matter how appealing it might otherwise be.

Advisors also need to be aware of special time commitments associated with various program choices. Hybertson, Hulme, Smith and Holton (1992) found that the factor most detrimental to an adult student's sense of wellness was feeling overwhelmed or conflicted about fulfilling responsibilities. Discovering how to manage their varied commitments represents a significant challenge to most adult learners.

Advisors should assist advisees in realistically assessing whether they can devote the time and energy required by a given program. Referring these learners to other adults who are currently pursuing the degree or who have recently completed it may help the student form a more realistic picture. Enrolled students who are finding it difficult to meet their multiple commitments may profit from a referral to time and stress management workshops.

Equally important at this step is encouraging students to be realistic. For example, if learners have consistently had difficulty with mathematics, a degree program that features competency in this discipline is not likely to prove viable. It is often helpful to encourage reality-testing of abilities needed to succeed in a given program. Referring advisees to graduates employed in a job for which the degree program was required may be a useful strategy. Such an interview can provide a realistic picture of the skills required on a daily basis, making possible a more accurate assessment of a learner's prospects for success in this field.

Information contained in college catalogues may be too brief to allow students to make an accurate program selection. In addition to encouraging interviews with alumni, advisors may want to suggest interviews with department faculty. Compiling a notebook containing job descriptions of previous graduates may also be a useful tool for enhancing the advisees' understanding of the degree programs they are considering. To initiate discussions regarding program choice, advisors may want to ask some of the following questions:

Questions To Encourage Advisees To Explore Program Choice

1. What majors are you currently considering?

2. What appeals to you about this degree?

3. Do you feel you have an accurate picture of what careers

this degree program can lead to and the challenges it might present?

4. What skills, abilities and values do you think this degree program might require, and how would you rank yourself in these areas?

5. Are there skill areas you would need to improve in order to be successful in this program?

6. Have you explored the labor market trends and how marketable this degree will be when you complete your degree?

7. How might family and work commitments interfere with your meeting the degree requirements?

8. Are there financial sacrifices you will have to make while completing this degree, and are you willing or capable of making these if required?

9. Of the required courses, which appeal to you the most? Least? Why?

10. What is the minimum grade point average for acceptance into the major? How realistic is it to maintain this average while responding to other life commitments?

Step 4. Choosing Courses

In Step 4, advisors seek to assist adult learners in selecting coursework. To be successful, advisors need to know what courses are available, when they are offered, what the prerequisites are, if they are transferable, and whether a given course helps meet graduation requirements. They also must understand rules and regulations related to probation and suspension and to course load limits. Advisors need to know about both remedial courses and honor courses. Although it is not always available, students often value information about course content and the instructor's teaching style.

Advisors of adult learners often face a disadvantage in initial advising sessions because little, if any, relevant information may be available about the learner's ability to perform in the classroom. Unlike traditional-age advisees, many adult learners enter college with outdated ACT scores and high school GPAs that may have little relevance for performance years later. In these instances, course placement (for example, in intermediate algebra versus college algebra) is often based on the students' self-assessment, a procedure that does not always provide an accurate picture of ability. Advisors may want to encourage students to take placement tests as an aid to course selection.

Some adult learners enter college with such limited skills and background that they require remediation in basic writing, reading, or computational skills, or all of these. Approximately 29% of first-year college students enroll in a remedial course. Of these, 46% were 22 years of age or older, and 25% were over 30 years old (*Chronicle of Higher Education*, 1998). These figures underscore the importance of encouraging adult learners to assess their current skill levels and to become aware of resources that can assist them in strengthening basic skills. For example, advisees who have consistently used math in their work may feel confident to enroll in college algebra. Those less secure in their math ability may need to explore refresher options, even though many institutions will not allow credit in such courses to apply toward graduation requirements.

Many older students feel a sense of urgency about completing their degrees in the shortest time possible. As a result, they become frustrated when they are asked to sit through courses in which they have already mastered the content. Advisors need to ask adult advisees to review their previous educational experiences. Many have experienced on-the-job training or have attended intensive workshops or seminars sponsored by their companies. Some will have extensive volunteer experience. Requesting adult advisees to submit an educational history can assist advisors in identifying experiences that may qualify for college credit. Therefore, advisors need to be aware of their institution's policies with respect to nonclassroom learning.

Nontraditional or alternative degree programs created for

adult learners frequently have well-established formal routines and policies for assessing and crediting prior learning. The majority of institutions, however, rely on traditional assessment methods such as departmental exemption tests and College Level Examination Program (CLEP) exams. In institutions where prior learning assessment has not been formalized or perhaps has even been discouraged, advisors can sometimes find routes by which this learning can be translated into college credit.

The benefits of prior learning assessment are many. With it, adult learners can begin their college experience at an appropriate point, and they also may experience an increased confidence in their ability to succeed because they see immediate progress.

Adults often become discouraged when their progress is impeded by constraints created by work and family demands. Such constraints limit the number of hours a learner can take, especially if their program offerings are restricted to face-to-face instruction. If scheduling problems, rather than available time, create the difficulty, advisors should help learners to explore alternative course formats.

An increasing number of higher education institutions have responded to adult learner needs by developing more flexible educational delivery systems. Although many adult learners will take the initiative in identifying coursework options, others will need their advisor's assistance to look beyond the on-campus "line schedule." An increasing number of courses are offered on the Web or through compressed video, interactive videoconferencing, cable television, audio- and videotape, and correspondence study. When exploring the availability of courses offered through these formats, it is desirable to encourage a discussion of learning style preferences and how these relate to available technology-based courses. Of course, advisors will need to inform advisees of policies that restrict course transferability and the number of technology-based courses allowed in each student's program.

Finally, some advisees will challenge the need for some required courses that may appear to be unrelated to the students' goals. In such instances, advisors should be able to provide the rationale for each required course and explain its pertinence to the students' lives. Advisors will need to help these adults see the broader application of the material. This often provides an opportunity to reinforce the importance of considering both short- and long-term goals when selecting coursework. The questions below can assist students in choosing courses:

Questions To Encourage Advisees To Explore Course Selection

1. How would you describe your experiences with school?

2. What strengths do you have now compared to when you were last enrolled?

3. What assets do you have that will assist you in succeeding? Liabilities?

4. What previous learning experiences (such as previous course-work, on-the-job training, or military) do you have, and how might those be useful to you?

5. In previous learning experiences, what did you find challenging, helpful, or distracting?

6. How confident are you in your ability to succeed in the courses you have selected?

7. Are there any specific subjects in which you anticipate difficulty? Do you think you will want or need tutoring assistance?

8. Can you identify any courses in which you might already possess the required knowledge base (perhaps through your work, training activities, or independent study)?

9. How comfortable would you be exploring possible departmental exams, standardized exams (such as CLEP), or other means by which to have this prior learning evaluated?

10. Do you prefer the personal interaction available through face-to-face courses, or would you like to explore alternative course formats to complete your required courses?

Step 5. Course Scheduling

Often considered to be the clerical function of academic advising, the course scheduling step can be very important to student success. Research on adult student enrollment patterns (Bonham & Luckie, 1993; Robertson, 1991) suggests that if adequate attention is not devoted to this step, student retention may be jeopardized.

Many adult students establish unrealistic time lines. Such advisees approach their education with a sense of urgency—a need to complete something they should have resolved years ago. This sense of urgency, combined with high expectations for achievement, creates an environment that threatens student success.

It is important that adult students be encouraged to take credit loads that enable them to succeed without neglecting other responsibilities. Advisors should help students set realistic schedules that consider commuting time as well as the time required to attend and prepare for courses. In this connection, advisors may want to discourage students from enrolling in multiple courses that require additional laboratory time.

As discussed in an earlier chapter, the enrollment pattern for many adult students is not continuous. Many stop out, intending to return at a later date. Academic advisors should take steps to assist the student in avoiding unnecessary stopouts. For example, potential stopout candidates may be encouraged to stay enrolled by taking lighter loads that reduce time and financial pressures.

If continuous enrollment is not a viable option for an adult, it is important that advisors provide guidance that can help the adult plan for reentry. For example, providing information about existing required course rotation plans can help advisees know when attendance is absolutely critical to their degree completion.

Advisors should recognize that many adult advisees may have little flexibility in their schedules. They often need to develop realistic, long-term plans that consider work and family commitments. The following questions can be asked to help determine course scheduling issues:

Questions To Encourage Advisees To Explore Course Scheduling Issues

1. How many hours per day are you planning to devote to class participation?

2. How many hours a week can you devote to preparing for class (doing homework assignments)?

3. Are there limitations as to the time of day or days of the week we need to work your class schedule around?

4. Assuming you live off-campus, how much time do we need to allow for commuting to and from class?

5. Are there transportation or child-care issues, or both, that we need to be concerned about as we formulate your schedule?

6. In addition to taking courses, what other commitments do you have that will take your time and energy?

7. How do your friends and family feel about your return to school?

8. What is the best way for me to reach you? Where and when is it most convenient for me to call should I need to do so?

9. Do you have questions or concerns about coursework or other matters that need to be answered?

CONCLUSION

Many advisors are often trained first as academicians. A few have specialized training in teaching. Hardly any receive training in advising. It is not surprising that being an effective advisor has not been a high priority for some individuals.

An increasing number of educators, however, view the purposes of higher education as much broader than the mastery of subject matter and accompanying skills. Promoting personal development—including self-awareness of abilities, interests, values, and relevance of these for lifelong decisions—is recognized as one of higher education's most important commitments. Education of this type is accomplished most effectively through person-to-person interactions. The advising setting provides the occasion for these interactions. Viewed in this light, advising is personal education; it provides the advisor with the opportunity to broaden the student's orientation and education. At the same time, when it is done well, it ensures that the student will arrive in structured learning situations in an optimum condition to learn.

Advising adult learners is no small challenge. Not all advisors will feel equipped to face these challenges single-handedly. A variety of campus resource people can assist advisors in addressing the various issues outlined in this chapter. All advisors should strive for the following outcomes: (a) helping students to set realistic goals that challenge them to work to their full potential, (b) helping students make connections between their life and career goals and their educational objectives, and (c) helping advisees become more effective at decision making, including the ability to deal knowledgeably and flexibly with transitions. Within a developmental framework, effective advisors challenge, support, and provide vision to the students with whom they work. The following checklist will assist advisors in assessing their readiness to assume this vital role:

Advisor Checklist

1. Are your advising hours and location compatible with the needs of adult learners?

2. Are adults able to confirm appointments in advance so if necessary they can make arrangements for child care, transportation, and work coverage in advance?

3. Do your advisees have access to advising by telephone, e-mail? What other technologies might be adopted to help adult students obtain information in a timely, efficient manner?

4. Are you aware of campus as well as community resources that might assist adult learners? Do you have a specific person you could contact if necessary?

5. During advising sessions, do you encourage advisees to focus on broader life planning issues?

6. Does the advising session allow enough time to explore issues beyond course selection?

7. What do you do to assist adults in making connections between their educational and vocational goals?

8. Are you aware of campus policies on prior learning assessment (PLA)? Do you know what types of assessment is available and where students should be referred? Do you know if your institution will transfer hours from PLA? Are there policies limiting the number of credits transferable from PLA?

9. Do you know alternative course formats available to students that might assist students who have many time and location constraints?

10. Are you familiar with theories about the developmental needs of adult students?

11. To what extent can you influence the curriculum and program offerings that may create barriers for adult learners?

12. What are the key retention issues and retention goals concerning adults at your institution? What role can you play as an advisor in addressing these retention issues and goals?

13. What institutional policies or procedures present barriers or inhibit the success of adult learners at your institution? What are solutions to these problems? What role can you play in addressing these issues?

14. As an advisor, how can you help adult students balance long-term educational needs with short-term goals?

15. Have you created an advisor in-take form that advisees can complete to assist you in addressing the unique challenges they may have in college attendance?

CHAPTER 5

Creating Community for Adult Learners

I tend to take everything with a grain of salt because I know what we're learning in school is book learning. It's not practical application outside the classroom. I'm only interested in what is real in the real world of work and life.—40-year-old student

I have been amazed at how college has changed my life, my way of seeing things. I pick up the newspaper and read things. I said, "Golly, it goes right along with the course I'm taking. This is weird and strange." And I find that I am getting my family involved and my friends with my readings and new ideas and ways of thinking and talking about what's going on. My learning is happening every day in my life.—38-year-old student

They really encourage team building. They force you to be in the team. They call it a study group, but to me it's a team. And it's an encouragement if I get stuck on a problem, I know I can call one of my study group people. We've become like a family. And we give each other support and positive strokes when the family or the work and the school stuff gets discouraging.—32-year-old student

Learning communities are important to adult students. These learning communities occur within an adult context that shapes their learning experiences. Although adult learners have a major part in identifying and selecting how they wish to participate in learning, the context of each learner's experience has an equally powerful part in defining the preferred learning goals, as well as the structure and process of learning. This context can expand and enhance the quality of the learning or limit the learner's involvement. For example, the learning experiences described by adults in the above quotes are each quite different. Yet, each of these quotes represent typical experiences for adult undergraduate students. These experiences are influenced by both the students' adult lives and their particular collegiate contexts.

THE IMPORTANCE OF
LEARNING COMMUNITIES

College leaders often assume that learning communities can occur only within the collegiate world. These beliefs have been supported by Astin's theory of involvement (1985) and Tinto's (1997) research on college persistence, suggesting the importance of social and intellectual learning involvement for learners within the collegiate environment. Although research based on studies of younger adult undergraduates supports these understandings, growing research on adult students suggest an expanded perspective. For adults, the primary learning community on the campus is within the classroom, with linkages to other significant learning communities of work, family, and community (Fishback, 1997; Kasworm & Blowers, 1994). Adult learners bring to college a number of important and sometimes competing formal and informal learning communities. Each of these communities can create learning connections between the classroom content and the multiple roles of the adult. They can also create important learning support structures. Some of these learning contexts, however, may be at odds with the mission and structure of the collegiate world and can deter learning. As a result, adult learners present new challenges to faculty and staff.

This broader perspective of adult learning communities is based in the theory of situated learning (Lave & Wenger, 1991; Wenger, 1998), which suggests that learning occurs in relation to the learner's background, the current context of the classroom and college learning experience, as well as the current adult life roles and circumstances. In situated learning, the learner's life context defines both the goals and interests of the learner, as well as his or her preferred type of learning experiences and involvement. It does makes a difference that the adult learner is a supervisor in an electric utility company, or a homemaker providing teacher aide support for a local school, or a contributor to a Habitat for Humanity community group. It does make a difference that adults can only participate in college courses during evenings, mornings, or weekends. Situated learning suggests that effective learning experiences support and connect the three elements of (a) the learner; (b) the learner's current roles of work, family, and community; and (c) the learner's participation in collegiate learning. This connection is also based on the belief that learners respond to learning communities through "authentic relationships," relationships that support and extend learning both within college and in adult lives. These relationships are fundamentally grounded in the belief that adults are valued learners. These relationships also provide the important structures and processes that support the adult's multiple worlds both within the college and within specific classroom experiences.

Situated learning theory considers two worlds: the collegiate world of the instructor, the curriculum, and the collegiate environment, and the learner's world of work, family, significant friendships, and community relationships. Each of these worlds has an impact upon the other, and upon the adult student's learning experience; both worlds represent many learning communities. Effective collegiate learning for adults integrates these multiple learning communities within the classroom and recognizes that often the most powerful learning outcomes occur beyond the classroom. Thus, the challenge for faculty and staff is to create effective adult learning communities both within and beyond the classroom that foster cognitive development, group and individual learning, intellectual growth, memory enhancement, and emotional satisfaction in the learning process (Bruffee, 1995; Gabelnich, MacGregor, Matthews, and Smith, 1990; Lenning & Ebbers, 1999; Shapiro & Levine, 1999; Strange & Banning, 2001; Wenger, 1998). Equally important, based on the authors' research and discussions with adult learners, effective collegiate learning communities create a personal joy in the learning process based on relevance, personal curiosity, and accomplishment in the adult world. Recent research studies also suggest that these significant learning communities support each adult's sense of being valued as a college student and support each adult's commitment to persist in completing a collegiate degree (Kasworm & Blowers, 1994).

The Connecting Classroom for Adults

The most potent learning community for adults in college is the *connecting classroom*, which represents the literal connection between the classroom world and the adult student's world (Graham, Donaldson, Kasworm, & Dirkx, 2000). The connecting classroom emphasizes the relationship between classroom experiences and adult lives, and that relationship's influence on how adult students connect learning to life meanings. For example, an adult student's experience of a new job assignment, a pending world crisis, or a community project to upgrade recreational areas can create a new awareness of course content and an urgency to learn it. That experience can also shape what the adult learner seeks out beyond the class text and discussions. In particular, recent research suggests that adult beliefs about the relevance and purposes of knowledge and its sources of authority influence adult engagement in or avoidance of specific learning experiences (Kasworm, 1997; Kasworm & Blowers, 1994).

Adult students have presented five different perspectives of their beliefs about the relevancy and purpose of knowledge and its sources of authority in their lives (Kasworm, 1997). These different perspectives (identified as *knowledge voices* by Kasworm) suggest that most adult students believe there are two worlds of knowledge authority, which influences their learning in the classroom. There is the "real" world of knowledge, directed at adults' daily actions in the world and used by adults to be competent and effective in their adult worlds. The second world is the "academic world of knowledge," knowledge that is defined through detailed theory, books, and discipline-related discussions evaluated in tests and papers. These five voices (Kasworm) represent five types of adult learners as they speak to their beliefs about engagement in learning (note Table 5.1).

Table 5.1. Adult Belief Structures of Knowledge Engagement

Belief Structure	Valued knowledge	Valued learning actions	Valued professor actions	Valued classroom activities	Valued evaluation strategies	Valued learning community
Entry Voice	Academic knowledge	How to be a successful student as judged by grades	Guiding students to become successful as judged by grades	Direct knowledge organization for memorization or/and providing learning how to learn skills	Clear evaluation strategies for students to show their success on tests and essays	Relationship is based in instructor actions to help the adult student get good grades and be successful.
Outside Voice	Real world knowledge	Reinforces current knowledge; Validates knowledge expertise	Creating learning based in the student's real world understandings; Valuing adult's real world expertise	Knowledge activities that reflects real world realities and future applications; Knowledge that helps them be more competent in the real world	Evaluation that demonstrates their real world applications and competencies	Real-world connected learning communities; classrooms based in real world applications
Cynical Voice	Cynical about value and relevance of academic knowledge	No valued learning activities. Participate as a necessary step to gain credential	Creating non-interactive and non-demeaning classroom and grading practices	Unobserved, uninvolved and isolated	Desire non-graded involvements or being judged successful in the classroom	No valuing of academic communities. Values real world

Continued on next page.

Table 5.1. *Continued*

Belief Structure	Valued knowledge	Valued learning actions	Valued professor actions	Valued classroom activities	Valued evaluation strategies	Valued learning community
Straddling Voice	Values both academic and real world knowledge	Creation of applications and connections between two knowledges and worlds	Creating learning which values both life worlds and both knowledge worlds	Experience active, collaborative, applied learning within classroom and across their adult life roles. Values synthesis and critique	Preferred evaluation that displays new understandings and applications between these two worlds	Engage in multiple learning communities within the classroom, through work, family, community, and self-defiend groups
Inclusion Voice	Values the academic world and the integration and creation of new knowledge across both world	Develop complex, multiple world-views and intellectual engagement in knowledge	Faculty as mentors and colleagues in the intellectual knowledge sharing and creation efforts	Experience theory and application; exploration of ideas of theory and beliefs; critical thinking and analysis.	Values intellectual creation through research papers, research projects, and independent readings.	Values the life of the mind and academic and real world communities that support that perspective

The first quote in this chapter presents one adult's belief about "book learning" versus knowledge of the world through practical applications. The second quote, through another adult's eyes, indicates that both knowledge worlds connect in meaningful ways. For these two adults and many others, these differences in perspective reflect basic beliefs about the relevancy of knowledge, the relevancy of learning goals for the adult and for the classroom instructor, and about related adult student preferences for a learning community. Although intellect and cognitive complexity do influence each adult learner's engagement in learning, these knowledge voices reflect the *stance* of the adult learner in relation to learning and are not necessarily influenced by the level of cognitive knowledge or reflective judgment (Baxter Magolda, 1992; Belenky, Clinchy, Goldberger, and Tarule, 1986; King & Kitchener, 1994; Perry, 1981).

Entry Voice

Type of adult student. This voice represents adult students who are new to the college classroom or those enrolled in a particular discipline unknown to them (such as a foreign language). These students view themselves as novices. They believe that they have no valued status and that their real world expertise is not valued or appropriate for use in their student learning role.

Basic belief. These adult students believe that they cannot judge the value of learning specific content, nor are they able to make personal sense of this classroom knowledge during their early courses. They don't perceive a relationship between most classroom learning and their current roles and life status. Therefore, they attempt to memorize all "appropriate" classroom knowledge. These adults believe that they will come to understand the importance of a specific class content later in their college work. They view faculty members as the ultimate expert, as all powerful, and often as god-like authorities.

Key learning goals. These students' central goal is to make good grades—to be successful in the student role. Most will concentrate on acquiring knowledge and skill to be that successful student. They want to learn how to be a good student by learning how to study, take tests, and write good papers. They assume that memorizing all the identified important knowledge *will be* important. They assume that classroom knowledge need not initially be relevant, applicable, and related to their adult life.

Desires for a learning community. Most of these adult students see little value in learning communities. Their chief concern is academic survival as defined by grades and by acquisition of status and credibility as a student.

Outside Voice

Type of adult student. This student voice represents adult students who are anchored within the adult world of work, family, and life external to the college setting. Such students stand inside their adult worlds and look to selective participation in the academic world of learning.

Basic belief. These adults value their real-world knowledge expertise and stand proudly within their current adult life status in work, family, and community. College is a necessary involvement for them. They view it as a unique and sometimes foreign culture, with only fragmentary connections to their world of work, family, and self. They generally appreciate their college experience, but are highly selective in what they consider as worthwhile learning. Faculty are judged on the basis of their attitudes toward adult students, the relevance of the class content to the students' adult life experiences, and the adult students' expertise in nonacademic worlds.

Key learning goals. These students value academic knowledge that comes from or is congruent with their understandings of their roles and responsibilities. They value classroom learning that extends and reinforces their current knowledge world, supports their self-image, or validates their expertise in real-world knowledge. Knowledge that is dissonant from their worldview may be acquired if the faculty member presenting it is highly supportive and skillful in efforts related to application, critique, and reflection. Typically, these adults seek out good grades in support of their life status and self-image as a competent professional. Their long-term learning, however, will be selective. If the content of a class is not anchored in their world, they will learn content for the test and the course grade; but it will be for short-term retention only.

Desires for a learning community. Students with this voice concentrate on learning that supports and enhances their current world of work, family, and community. Learning communities based on adult circumstances, adult careers, and adult applications will be valued. These students will also value classes and faculty that require discussion, projects, or activities that integrate academic and real-world knowledge.

Cynical Voice

Type of adult student. This voice represents adult students who present an implicitly cynical or antagonistic involvement in college learning. Through a variety of circumstances, these students see themselves forced into the college student experience. Although doubtful of the inherent value of the college experience, they believe they must gain a credential to provide them with legitimacy and access to preferred jobs, employment privileges, and societal status.

Basic belief. The classroom is a charade. These students see themselves forced into participation to gain acceptable grades, the requisite credit hours, and the college credential. They dislike and fear faculty, judging them to be manipulative, incompetent, arrogant, or naive.

Key learning goals. These adult students believe that, at best, there may be limited value in learning collegiate information. They actively discriminate and put down most instruction and content as useless. They present external compliance to get an acceptable grade, but are often antagonistic or cynical in their interactions. Their learning is only for the test and the grade. Most of these students do not excel with course grades; therefore, they also feel put-down by the instructor and the academic environment. They present a variety of strategies to hide, disengage, or protect themselves from the perceived cruel or irrelevant world of academic learning and its grading system.

Desires for a learning community. These adult students emphasize their own real-world expertise. They desire no connection with the academic world.

Straddling Voice

Type of adult student. This voice represents adult students who value learning from both the academic world and the adult world. These adult learners believe that the world of academic learning is valuable in its own right, but they also believe it can enhance their real-world understandings and actions. Most of these adult students have had prior college experiences; have engaged in self-directed learning through reading, traveling, or community efforts; or have participated in work and community groups composed of college-educated colleagues.

Basic belief. These adults seek out both worlds to gain knowledge and to inform them of other world understandings, perspectives, and actions. They exhibit openness, curiosity, and active learning. Although they may not initially value liberal studies or lower division education for their day-to-day lives, these students will later report satisfaction with the value of these ideas, principles, and understandings to their lives.

Key learning goals. These adults actively engage in classroom activities. They often are involved in two "channels" of learning. One channel seeks to learn and understand the academic knowledge in its own right; the other channel seeks to understand its implications for real-world knowledge. In addition, they seek through both introspection and action to make connections between the "academic" and "real" worlds. They value faculty members who create classroom experiences in application, synthesize, and critique across these two worlds of knowledge. They believe that most faculty value adult student real-world expertise and that some of these faculty can skillfully use this real-world expertise to enrich the understanding of academic knowledge.

Desire for a learning community. These students value faculty and students who explore and critique knowledge by applying it to the real world. Because they see a separation of these two knowledge worlds, they create their own learning groups and participate in learning communities within their worlds of work, community, and family, as well as within the college learning communities.

Inclusion Voice

Type of adult student. This voice represents adult students who are actively immersed in the academic world and in the intellectual life of the academy. Because they have multiple worldviews beyond the notions of two knowledge sources (real-world and academic), they consider the college class through multiple understandings of each of their various life roles and responsibilities. They have a deep commitment to the intellectual journey. Most of these adult students are open to or committed to future graduate studies. Many have an interest in becoming faculty members, even though they question that possibility because of their age, work, and life circumstances.

Basic belief. These adults perceive themselves as building bridges between their worlds outside the academy and within the academy. They integrate thought and action through these two worlds, but prefer to look at themselves and their worlds through intellectual frameworks. For them, the classroom is one of a number of learning engagements in their intellectual development. Faculty are viewed as fellow experts and colleagues.

Key learning goals. Learning for these adults is personally defined. The classroom is one of many tools for exploring new knowledge, understandings, and possibilities. All knowledge is viewed as conceptual; thus, at minimum, they see themselves integrating knowledge from both the real and the academic worlds. They often create and transform knowledge into personally defined new meanings and applications. These adults are attracted to the life of the mind and engage in learning for learning's sake. They value independent projects and research that allows them to explore new learning.

Desire for a learning community. These adults readily participate in a broad range of learning communities. But they place the greatest value on experiences and relationships that facilitate the development of knowledge, skills, and actions valued in the academy.

Implications for the Connecting Classroom

Adults' beliefs about their knowledge expertise and the purpose of knowledge influence their involvement in the classroom and in campus-related activities. Faculty members need to understand the current beliefs of their adult students so that they can create multiple strategies to support and broaden each adult student's experiences. Based on this descriptive typology, the following general strategies suggest ways to support the key learning goals and beliefs of these varied learners.

Strategies for Entry Students

The Entry Voice, which represents most entry and some reentry adult students, requires strategies that foster success in developing effective study skills and in creating socializing experiences within the classroom. As noted in Chapter 3, academic and student affairs professionals can create a variety of entry workshops, orientation sessions, and first-year courses that provide adults with knowledge and skills to be successful as students. Faculty members need to provide initial messages to adult students confirming their value and worth, and to show confidence that the students can be successful in the college setting. Adults need feedback early in the semester about their academic progress and about ways to improve their academic performance. These adult students appreciate faculty who provide guidelines, examples, and tips for successful note-taking, study techniques, classroom assignments, library research, and written exams. Faculty should understand that many of these students are experiencing college life for the first time. They need faculty support that engages them in learning.

Strategies for Adults in the "Real World"

Three of the voices, the Outside Voice, the Cynical Voice, and the Straddling Voice, are based in the dominant world of adult life outside of college. For these adult learners, faculty should design instructional strategies, programs, and services that proactively relate academic content to adult roles of work, family and community. Academic programs and institutions may wish to design options that serve adults in specific roles, such as adult degree programs, professional degree programs, or worksite course offerings.

In many instances, adults anchored in their adult worlds are participating in general education lower division courses, as well as in age-integrated courses and programs. Faculty and student affairs staff need to craft learning experiences that actively draw upon adult life experiences and the real-world expertise of their students. Principles and program designs for integrating adult life roles and experiences into course content, activities, and learning designs are suggested in later sections of this chapter. In addition, faculty and student affairs staff are encouraged to establish personal relationships with these adult students to better understand adult beliefs and their learning patterns. Faculty and staff can sometimes engage adult students in mutually agreeable ways to enrich the course through real-world involvement. For example, one faculty member negotiated an action-learning project in environmental management with an adult student as a stimulating substitute to a traditional library research project.

It is important for faculty and staff to recognize that these three groups often reflect adult students who are more likely to fail or drop out, who can't see the relevance of college, or who lose their interest in and commitment to pursuing a college degree. Personal knowledge and relationships with such students can forestall these disappointments. Additional discussions relative to techniques for providing student support and encouraging socialization are found in Chapter 4 on academic advising and Chapter 6 on adult student services.

Strategies for Adult Students in the Academic World

Faculty and student affairs staff have a natural affinity for adult students who have either an Inclusion Voice—those who value or wish to live in the academic world. It would be a mistake, however, to assume that these adult students would be well served by learning approaches and programs designed for young college students. These adults want to participate in courses, academic programs, and student activities that are relevant and meaningful, that are offered on a convenient schedule, and that convey an understanding of and support for adult students. For these students, faculty need to create academic programs and instructional activities that maximize the connections between the academic world and these students' complex life experiences and relationships. Adult students value academic learning communities that build upon those connections.

Because of their personal investment in the academic world, these adults also are more likely to selectively engage in cocurricular activities and occasionally extracurricular activities. Faculty and staff can identify additional possibilities by involving adult students in advisory groups or focus groups. Such involvements often generate suggestions for new programs, supports, and services. Adult learners who value the academic world are more likely to react positively to special opportunities to participate in specific academic projects and relationships—for example, a faculty research project, an honorary society, an exhibit, a collateral program, or a tour. Such students usually appreciate an opportunity to learn about new books or journal articles on topics of interest. Frequently, they will seek to establish personal relationships with faculty or student affairs staff as a way to develop further understandings of the academic world. Adult students in this knowledge voice are remarkable for following their intellectual interests. For example, one adult created a family vacation and also crafted key readings to enrich their exploration of ancient cities of Greece and Italy. These students present particularly intriguing stories of their personal involvement in college and its impact upon their current and future lives. In the remainder of this chapter, we will explore principles and strategies that can create learning communities to build upon these intellectual interests of adult students.

CREATING LEARNING COMMUNITIES

Creating learning communities for adults represents a difficult, but important challenge for faculty and staff. It is not a simple matter of "placing" adults within a classroom or a group. Rather, these communities are created through significant relationships and services, as well as quality learning experiences supportive of adults as workers, family members, and community citizens.

A variety of strategies are required to meaningfully engage a diverse set of adults in learning that is applicable both within and beyond the academic world. Successful efforts to build learning communities recognize that adult students value a collaborative climate of peer learners and faculty, and that classes are energized when individuals come to know and value one another's perspectives and life experiences. Many current designs for adult learner communities have been inspired by studying young college student learning communities. Shapiro and Levine (1999), Lenning and Ebbers (1999), and MacGregor, Cooper, Smith, and Robinson (2000) offer a number of ideas adaptable to adult learner groupings. Because the diversity of adult learners requires a broad repertoire of relational, instructional, curricular, support service, and policy strategies, this section will present key frameworks for considering various strategies. Establishing community connections through face-to-face classrooms will be discussed in depth. With these understandings of the instructional learning process for adults, other key instructional delivery formats that establish learning community connections can be highlighted.

Face-to-Face Classroom Strategies for a Connecting Classroom

Face-to-face adult learning environments reflect purposeful planning to move beyond a classroom of passive, anonymous students who experience a lecture. In the connecting classroom, an environment exists that brings together the best psychological, physical, social, and intellectual aspects of an effective learning climate. It presents the combining of each adult's academic world and his or her world of adult roles and commitments.

Psychological Climate

The psychological climate of the classroom is a major factor in supporting adult learning. Guiding principles for designing an adult-responsive climate include the following:

Establishing Individual Identity. From the first entry by the adult into the classroom, each faculty member is urged to provide a climate of familiarity, if not friendship, for each student. Typically, one effort is to create a student roster with names and e-mail addresses or phone numbers, or both. Work-site information might also be provided. First-day class activities would include introductions, including brief biographical sharing through either small groups or the entire class. If appropriate technology is available, a class Web presence with digital photos, background information, and e-mail addresses would be of value. Obviously, student rights to privacy must be protected; but in most courses and with most students, establishing a personal class identity is a welcome way to set up a connecting classroom. Students need to discover a basis for relating to others socially in the classroom and in support groups. Faculty members should also share enough of their identity to show how their background might connect with the students' backgrounds.

Creating openness and trust. Faculty establish student expectations for the level and quality of participation. They determine whether or not there will be candid sharing and personal revelations within the classroom. Those faculty who focus solely upon content communicate that the class is not a place to individually explore the personal meaning of the ideas and concepts being presented. A psychological climate that encourages such sharing, however, assumes that learning is a social and a moral act, as well as a cognitive exercise. In the connecting classroom, adults need to feel that their adult worlds beyond the classroom are valued and respected. If faculty present themselves as authentic individuals, they will show a caring attitude and a desire for the adult students to interpret class content in the context of their personal situations (Brookfield, 1990). A desired faculty goal should be to present themselves as open and trusting of the students and of each student's private world of ideas, questions, and possibilities in the classroom.

Valuing, modeling, and critiquing. In the early classes of any course, it is important for faculty to establish ground rules for intellectual engagement in the course content. They need to model acceptable ways to confront controversial ideas and to critique reasoning. This effort represents a profound faculty responsibility. Many adult students are not able to detach themselves from specific ideas, values, and beliefs that are under discussion. For a number of them, the validity of their real-world expertise may be threatened. Yet higher education stresses the development of higher order thinking skills. The task is made easier by faculty who model a safe environment for critically reflecting upon adult beliefs and values. Faculty members need to develop a finely tuned reading of an individual student's capacity to deal with incongruity between course content and personal beliefs. Faculty are challenged to provide a model that encourages individuals and groups to explore differing or conflicting worldviews in a nonjudgmental fashion.

Learning through and with others. Many adult students come to the classroom through individual efforts and sacrifices. Some are so self-reliant that they border on dogmatic individualism, posing an obstacle to connecting learning. Adult students need to come to value the diversity of adults through their perspectives and experiences. Faculty can help students to understand the value of learning through others. Specific instructional strategies are discussed later in this section under intellectual climate.

These dimensions of a classroom's psychological climate are discussed in a number of recent books. The authors suggest examining Cross's *Adults As Learners* (1981), Wlodkowski's *Enhancing Adult Motivation to Learn* (1999), Wlodkowski and Ginsberg's *Diversity and Motivation* (1995), Brookfield's *The*

Skillful Teacher: On Technique, Trust and Responsiveness in the Classroom (1990), Merriam and Caffarella's (1999) *Learning in Adulthood*, and Hayes and Flannery's (2000) *Women as Learners*.

Physical Climate

Faculty often face the special challenge of working with adult students' physical limitations. Currently 40% of college students with a disability are 25 years of age or older (NCES, June, 2000). Older adults are more likely to have diminished sight and hearing due to aging. Thus, serving adults requires alertness to the physical climate of learning. Most adults will actively accommodate their learning needs when given the opportunity to sit closer or to alert the faculty member to their special learning needs.

Faculty have little control over many aspects of the physical classroom environment, frequently facing aged facilities, background noise, and cramped seating. Yet, knowing that learning occurs in supportive spaces, many faculty members attempt to establish a physical climate that can maximize adult learning. Because adult student energy levels often sag after a full day of work or family, these adults also desire a physical climate that is energized and engaging. Using multimedia strategies—such as well-designed overheads, written case study handouts, music, or videotape sharing—can provide variety and interest, as well as help to address the physical limitations of the environment. In addition, employing varied instructional activities for a physical and psychological change of pace, such as small group breakouts, can soften the varied physical challenges faced by adult students. For example, one adult student noted that he felt like a prisoner sitting still in a chair for two hours. He appreciated it when his instructor gave him a break to stretch and get his "blood flowing again."

There is much debate about the design of effective physical learning environments. Depending upon class size and the placement of classroom seating, seating placement in a U-shape maximizes opportunities to see members of the class, and thus enhances the physical sense of learning community. Adult students also appreciate flexible classroom seating that provides opportunities for small group discussions. Adults often look at traditional lecture halls as an arena for cattle-herding. They have preferences for classrooms with tables that give them a place to open and review a text, take notes, and use laptops. They also prefer classrooms that allow for drinks and snacks. After a full day of work, many have no time for dinner before attending a two- to three-hour evening class.

Faculty can facilitate the group dynamics of a connecting classroom by observing and modifying the physical placement of classroom seating, providing variety in classroom exercises, and embedding adult-to-adult interactions in class activities. More detailed background on the physical environment for adult learning can be found in Hiemstra and Sisco's (1990) *Individualizing Instruction: Making Learning Personal, Empowering, and Successful* and Hiemstra's (1991) *Creating Environments for Effective Adult Learning*.

Social Climate

Because learning is a social act, faculty need to develop individual-to-group connections as part of the course. Although some faculty may believe that this role reaches beyond their responsibilities, it cannot be neglected if one is committed to creating a connecting classroom environment. Faculty can foster a positive social climate by employing instructional strategies that build relationships. When an effective group climate exists, group learning is facilitated by effective collaborative learning. As part of this process, opportunities should be provided to explore the diversity of adult student experiences in relation to class content. This diversity will be evident not only in age, experience, and maturity levels of students in the classroom but also in the personalized meanings of the course relative to the students' worlds of work, family, and community.

A classroom with an effective social environment moves beyond developing opportunities to share individual and group experiences. Adults respond to a classroom environment that acknowledges significant life events, such as the birth of a child or a marriage. For example, one dislocated worker who shared his plight with a class received understanding and support while completing his final course and accolades when he accepted a new position that promised to use both his past work experiences and his recent academic background. Beyond these personal life events, the class as a learning community may also institute social rituals that support the adult experience. A faculty member can initiate a mid-term pizza party, an end-of-semester potluck, or an end-of-course celebration at a local college hangout to promote continued learning connections. Some adult students gather either before or after a class to eat, drink, or talk about the class and their lives. And some adults will purposefully plan future joint course enrollments seeking these social involvements.

Resources that will help faculty members understand and take advantage of the social climate's impact on learning include Wlodkowski and Ginsberg's (1995) *Diversity and Motivation: Culturally Responsive Teaching*, Polson's (1993) *Teaching Adult Students*, Daloz's (1999) *Mentor: Guiding the Journey of Adult Learners*, and Tisdell's (1995) *Creating Inclusive Adult Learning Environments*.

Intellectual Climate

Because adult learning consists largely of constructing and transforming knowledge and understanding, faculty members need to understand the intellectual involvement of adult students. Course designs that make intellectual connections between course content and the adults' knowledge of their other worlds have a potent impact on learning. Within the course design, adults need support for their beliefs about knowledge expertise. These supports include the desire to be successful students, the desire to have their real world valued in the academic world, and the desire to more fully relate the academic world to work, family, and community.

The adult classroom should encourage collaboration between faculty and adult learners (Knowles, 1980; Bruffee, 1995).

The teacher can serve to translate the content, communicate the language and rules of the academic discipline, and mentor higher order thinking. In this process, the student critically examines both personal and professional assumptions, leading to possible transformative learning experiences. The instructor uses the learning community to actively support new understandings, alternative perspectives, and synergistic reinforcement of important class content (Cranton, 1994; Mezirow et al., 1991, 1999).

An effective adult intellectual climate is also based on a variety of instructional strategies that maximize knowledge organization, integrate adult beliefs and experiences, and foster group interaction. A large repertoire of instructional strategies can support a connecting classroom and a collaborative learning environment. These strategies could include small group techniques, such as break-out discussions of problem-posing questions; case studies; simulation games; in-class application exercises; role-play activities; or small group vignette discussions that solicit alternative student experiences related to major principles or applications. Other active instructional strategies could include debates, brainstorming and related creativity exercises, questioning strategies, and learning agendas based on a key outline of course content. Instructors can also create instructional strategies that move beyond the boundaries of the classroom, such as learning contracts, interviews and other out-of-class data collection techniques, and application projects related to the adult world.

The effective instructor chooses instructional strategies that authentically reflect support for the adult learners, while at the same time challenging the learner with new ways of understanding both of the worlds that make up his or her reality. Resources to further explore this topic include Angelo and Cross's (1993) *Classroom Assessment Techniques*, Galbraith's (1998) *Adult Learning Methods*, and (1991) *Facilitating Adult Learning: A Transactional Process*, Pratt's (1998) *Five Perspectives on Teaching in Adult and Higher Education*, Brookfield's (1987) *Developing Critical Thinkers: Challenging Adults to Explore Alternative Ways of Thinking and Acting*, Mezirow et al.'s (1991) *Fostering Critical Reflections in Adulthood: A Guide to Trans-*

formative and Emancipatory Learning, and (1999) *Learning As Transformation,* Cranton's (1994) *Understanding and Promoting Transformative Learning,* Taylor and Associates'(2000) *Developing Adult Learners,* and Tennant and Pogson's (1995) *Learning and Change in the Adult Years.*

Clustering Courses and Support Services

Among the academic strategies that can help to develop intentional learning communities, one of the more effective efforts brings together support services and specific courses into a learning community design. One major version of intentional adult learning communities is based on programmatic clustering of courses directed to lower-division or pre-entry adult students. These efforts may include tracks of two or more courses that meet lower division requirements, small class sizes, student cohort groups, and careful scheduling to meet adult student time requirements. There are also growing numbers of upper division curricula directed to adults with most of these elements. As one example, Keene State College (Keene, New Hampshire) recently implemented this strategy for preadmit students. They offer two credit courses taught on the same evening: College Success Strategies from 4:30 to 5:30 and, after an hour break for dinner, English 101 from 6:30 to 9:30. After the first study class session, the class is treated to dinner in the student union. The College Success Strategies class features assistance with note-taking, text reading, and test anxiety, as well as time management. Learning styles, assertiveness skills, relaxation techniques, and coping skills are also featured. The Counseling Center and Math Center, as well as other campus agencies that provide academic and student services supports, are involved as well as preadmission class facilitators.

East Tennessee State University (Johnson City, Tennessee) has also created a learning community designed to address the needs of working adults. A group of newly admitted adult students choose to participate in cohort-based general education courses. In addition, students participate in a one-credit-hour section of "College Adjustment" for enhancing study skills; they all work with the same academic advisor, and they experience coordinated instruction by faculty across the classes.

Adult Program Student Cohorts

Another form of intentional adult learning community features adult degree completion programs pursued by student cohorts. These cohort-based programs often offer opportunities to develop community relationships, integrated support services, and an accelerated schedule. Baker University (Baldwin City, Kansas), Columbia Union College (Takoma Park, Maryland), Northwestern College (St. Paul, Minnesota), Park College (Parkville, Missouri), Tusculum College (Greenville, Tennessee), and Thomas More College (Crestview Hills, Kentucky) are but a few of the institutions that have implemented adult cohort degree completion programs. These degree programs typically are offered in the evening, often in an accelerated course format; targeted to upper-division, work-related majors; and combined with other related adult academic supports such as portfolio assessment, student cohort advisory committees, and program academic advisors. Kasworm and Blowers (1994) have shown that these cohort experiences were judged by the participating adults to be highly effective for both their learning and for their psychological well-being. Students believed that these intact student-cohort communities were the major component for supporting their persistence and their success. A detailed discussion of adult cohort programs and related instructional designs is presented in Maehl's *Lifelong Learning at Its Best: Innovative Practices in Adult Credit Programs* (2000).

Crafting Community in Self-Directed Adult Degree Offerings

A third academic strategy for intentional adult learning communities centers on adult students seeking self-directed degree formats. These programs—often targeted to general studies degrees or self-defined programs—offer independent study

opportunities through print, video, or audio materials; learn-
ing-contract-based programs; or cyberspace distance learning
programs. These varied academic outreach programs require
curricula and academic support services that are holistically
planned for content, connectedness, delivery, and service to the
adult learner.

Recognizing the difficulties of students in more unstruc-
tured and distant environments, the planners of these programs
typically implement strategies designed to prepare students for
self-directedness in their collegiate studies, such as crafting materials and assignments that engage students in applying content
and gaining feedback. Successful programs recognize the importance of learning style preferences in the instructional design. They also provide support and feedback assistance at both
an academic and at a personal level.

The University of Oklahoma's bachelor of liberal studies
degree program (Norman, Oklahoma) offers several options
that embrace intentional classroom connectedness. (The Web
site for the program offers detailed information <http://www.
ou.edu/cls>.) In the bachelor of liberal studies/classic degree
program offered by the University of Oklahoma, the dominant
delivery system consists of independent readings, extensive writing and research assignments, and comprehensive exams with
brief intensive seminars on campus. Students may opt to complete a capstone experience that includes a 10-day on-campus
seminar and a senior thesis project. In another program option,
bachelor of liberal studies/Internet-guided interdisciplinary
studies (B.L.S/IGIS), a virtual classroom environment is created
through the use of Internet course ware. Participants receive
curricular materials from the Internet, conduct research on-line,
and submit assignments via e-mail. They participate in real-time
discussions, as well as asynchronous bulletin discussions with
classmates. These students also occasionally attend seminars on
campus related to the Internet-guided seminars. For this option,
both on-campus and virtual interactions are used to create student community, while the instructional design of the program
connects learning with work, family, and community. For this
kind of self-directed learning curricula to succeed, the partici-

pating students must have the clear and distinctive feeling that a learning community is being created. Additional discussion of individualized and self-directed learning formats is found in *Lifelong Learning at Its Best* (Maehl, 2000).

Community Connectedness in Cyberspace

One of the fastest growing arenas of adult learning is technology-supported formats. Almost 90% of institutions with enrollments of 10,000 or more are offering some form of Web-based education (Palloff & Pratt, 1999). This delivery format, together with other self-directed learning components, challenges many of our assumptions about learning communities and the connecting classroom. As noted in the above example from the University of Oklahoma, the Internet offers exciting new capabilities for creating a virtual-classroom learning community. Since virtual students do not experience a face-to-face classroom community, principles to guide the creation of on-line community and an adult learning climate are extremely important (Palloff & Pratt, 1999).

It is evident that the instructor has significantly more responsibility for establishing specific structures and processes within a virtual classroom than in a regular classroom. Even though learners do not meet face-to-face, they need to become acquainted with each other through initial introductions and through learning how to interact effectively and appropriately in this new medium. Group activities should be designed that allow learners to mutually explore and reflect on their experiences and that give them an opportunity to examine the implications of their learning for their multiple roles.

Concordia University (St. Paul, Minnesota) provides an on-line program that works to create community in several ways. Students must attend a four-day orientation program on campus at the beginning of course work. During this orientation, learners are introduced to classmates, faculty, and administrative staff involved with the program. Representatives from campus offices—such as the learning center, the virtual library, the counseling center, and the financial aid office—attend the orientation to answer questions and inform students about how to gain access to their services at a distance. The practitioners involved in the orientation assess each learner's computer skills and explain the technical aspects of the program. Students who have been in the program speak to new students informally about the experience of managing life and school, offering practical tips and encouragement. Class times are synchronized each week to further enhance a sense of belonging to a "real" classroom. Bulletin boards and chat rooms also serve to increase communication and dialogue among learners.

Many program leaders are exploring new ways to provide support services in these cyberspace classrooms. One excellent example is the University of Maryland's University College's "Bachelor's Degrees at a Distance" (College Park, Maryland). Through both a student program bulletin and a Web site, the program's facilitators delineate policies, curricula, and support services to help adult learners enter, participate, and connect this cyberspace enterprise with their current adult worlds of work, family, and community. An especially intriguing student support service is their on-line career services center.

A growing number of excellent books offer advice about developing cyberspace communities, including *Building Learning Communities in Cyberspace* by Palloff and Pratt (1999) and Kruger's (2000) chapter on "Using Information Technology to Create Communities of Learners."

CONNECTING CLASSROOMS AND ADULT LIVES

As suggested earlier in this chapter, effective adult learning communities require more than action by faculty and student affairs staff in the collegiate world. They require connectedness to the adult worlds of work, family, and community. For faculty and student affairs staff, this emphasis on a student's life away from the campus may appear incongruent with the perceived scope of their collegiate responsibilities. But when one considers the potency of the connecting classroom for learning and the elements that create such an experience, it is clear that everyone has an important role to play. If higher education institutions are serious about serving adult students, they must seek effective answers to the following question: "How can our programs and services be more closely connected and supportive of the work site, the family, and the community where the adult resides?"

CHAPTER 6

Student Services: Planning for the Adult Student

When I attended orientation, I was surrounded by 18-year-olds, and the focus seemed to be on how to get tickets for the football games and the dangers of binge drinking or how to avoid gaining the "freshmen fifteen pounds." They talked about leaving home and how to handle our new freedom; I left home 20 years ago. —38-year-old student

Going back to school was terrifying. I don't think that's an uncommon feeling. When you've been out of school for a while, you question yourself: Am I up to this? Can I still study? Can I retain things? Are my brain cells shot? Am I just too old for this? —45-year-old student

I just started taking classes. I knew I wanted a better life, but I didn't know what I wanted to do. I was into my second semester when my friend told me about the career-counseling center. Early guidance would have made a real difference. —30-year-old student

College and university educators have long recognized that students are made up of more than their intellects and that their capacity to profit from the higher education experience depends on a host of circumstances beyond those associated with the classroom. As a consequence, most institutions offer a comprehensive set of student services. The impetus for establishing student service programs has been the recognition that student needs, when unmet, undermine opportunities to succeed—not only in the classroom but also in the broader student development process designed to improve self-understanding and one's potential for life-long satisfaction.

The quotations at the beginning of this chapter make it clear that older students bring with them a unique set of special needs. If an institution is to meet these needs, those responsible for student affairs need to be aware of them, willing to address them, and creative in designing services that respond to them.

After years of interaction with 18- to 23-year-olds, student affairs personnel have a great deal of experience in planning programs that meet the needs of "traditional" students. This is apparent in the content of student services journals, the profession's literature, and major conferences that feature discussions of issues affecting the younger student. Although many publications often include an obligatory statement or paragraph noting the increasing adult population, they provide few suggestions for addressing the needs of these students. Because the professional literature offers little guidance on adult students, graduate programs preparing professionals for student affairs work offer limited information regarding adult learners.

This chapter attempts to offer some practical guidelines to assist in making student services more responsive to the adult student. The emphasis will be on areas of greatest significance to adult students where adults may require services differing from those provided for younger students. Areas to be examined include orientation, academic and learning assistance, career counseling, personal counseling, and student organizations.

UNIQUE CHARACTERISTICS REQUIRE UNIQUE STUDENT SERVICE RESPONSES

In order to serve adult students, program offerings may need to extend beyond those serving full-time, residential students. Schooling makes up only one of many tasks that adults face. Often patterns of class attendance revolve around work. Many adults attend classes at night or on weekends. Others come on campus, attend class, and leave immediately, returning to other responsibilities. Some adults attend class at satellite locations, and others take classes via the Internet and spend little or no time on campus.

Although many of the services for younger students may also assist adults, to assume that "one size fits all" ignores the fact that 18-year-olds and 30-year-olds are likely to be very different. For example, the counseling needs of the older adult student may revolve around family concerns and issues. While the traditional aged student may also enter the counseling center to deal with relationship issues, they are less likely to present challenges created by children and a spouse. When the adult student concerns require the expertise of a marriage and family therapist, counseling centers whose staff does not include one may need to help the adult student seek help outside the institution. Even when the counseling services sought by these learners are readily available on campus, they may prefer to meet their counseling needs in the local community and thus need referral assistance. Providing resources to ease adults during the entry period as well as throughout their tenure with the institution may mean the difference between success and failure.

As well as having been away from school longer than younger students, adults are also motivated differently. Participation studies clearly show that for adults, life transitions or employment-related issues often influence their decisions. Some major disruption in the adult's life may have occurred—death of a spouse, divorce, or loss of a job. Perhaps, the motivation to return is triggered by dissatisfaction with a current job, or the lack of promotion opportunities. Therefore, many adult students must navigate through a destabilized period in their lives and careers, a fact that may increase their need for career or personal counseling.

It is unwise for an adult educator or counselor to assume that adults have well-identified career goals when they enter higher education. Although some adults enter college with clear-cut career goals, those goals are not always based on a realistic understanding of the career to which they aspire. Adults usually have more work experience than younger students, but they often need help in identifying how the skills they have developed might transfer to other careers. They may even be unable to articulate the skills they have developed. Career counseling for adults thus takes on a different emphasis than the same service directed to recent high school graduates; it can provide a bridge between past work experience and potential future work.

Astin (1993) has shown that student involvement and interaction on campus play an integral role in student learning. The reality of adult lives often leaves little time to participate in student activities and organizations. In addition, activities planned with younger students in mind often have little appeal to adults. Although adult students' involvement on campus primarily centers around faculty and fellow students, student affairs personnel can increase the likelihood that adults will benefit from participating in campus activities through personal encouragement and by providing opportunities of special interest to adults. Adults as well as younger students benefit from on-campus involvement, but special effort must be made to ensure that adult students have access to such benefits.

Adult students have taken a giant leap of faith in themselves and their abilities to succeed despite the obstacles that their complex lives present. They have expectations that the system of higher education will help them to craft a better life for themselves and their families. Student affairs personnel, by understanding the needs of adults and considering those needs in program planning, can significantly improve the adult student's prospects for success and growth.

STRATEGIES FOR RESPONDING

Student affairs personnel will need to implement numerous strategies to ensure that services are available to adult students, especially those located off-campus. Ideally, campus offices will provide extended hours, at least during critical periods (such as pre-enrollment), and remain open over the lunch hour. Making services available via phone during evening hours or on Saturday would be beneficial to those off-campus. Some satellite programs have a site coordinator who provides administrative functions at off-campus locations. For example, the St. Francis College (Loretto, Pennsylvania) has a student location coordinator at each of their off-campus locations who contacts each new student, receives and sells textbooks in the classroom, and sets up class telephone lists. The location coordinator provides on-site support to faculty and students.

Many programs provide student services support on-line: Registration, class scheduling, and financial transactions can then take place when it is convenient for adults. The State University of New York at Stony Brook provides advising on-line and through telecounseling, fax, and e-mail. At Highland Community College in Freeport, Illinois, students can order books and course materials on-line as well as access admissions, counseling, financial aid, academic support services, and the library. When properly designed, on-line services can help adults save time and alleviate some of the frustrations associated with their inability to access student services face-to-face. For example, institutions that provide financial aid information on-line can offer customized assistance by listing scholarships defined by relevant features (scholarships for part-time students, community-based scholarships, and curriculum specific scholarships).

Web pages devoted to adult students can be created that highlight information about student services pertinent to adults and provide details of campus events of interest to adult students. An adult student Web page can serve as an on-line one-stop information center discussed later in this chapter. It may be helpful to design this Web page around the "moving-in," "moving-through," and "moving-out" concepts discussed by Schlossberg, Lynch, and Chickering (1989) by dividing the page into student services and information needed by adult students at various stages of their higher education experience. Polson (2000) provides a model for establishing a Web page based on this concept.

Relying solely on computer technology for information transfer, however, is unwise. Citing a 1998 campus computing survey, Gilbert (1998) reported that 45% of students at four-year institutions used the Internet at least once a day, but the comparable figure for community college students was 29%. Adults make up a large portion of community college student populations, and they are frequently less comfortable with technology than younger students. Providers cannot assume adults will have the skills or the equipment required to utilize computerized resources. Offering numerous options for reaching information must be made available.

Numerous publications offer examples of innovative ways

to deliver student services and ways to inform adults about the services available (National Clearinghouse for Commuter Programs, 1993 & 1998; College Board Office of Adult Learning Services, 1997). Bowling Green State University's Off-Campus Students Center (Bowling Green, Ohio) has initiated a quick response form that gives the Center's personnel authority to act on the student's issues identified on the form. The next business day, one of the Center's staff members pursues the student's request and makes a phone call to the student reporting the outcome. This service alleviates the need for working students to take vacation time to address relatively trivial university-related concerns. At Southwest Missouri State University in Cape Girardeau, Missouri, the bursar's office has provided automated teller machines that allow students to pay bills from their cars. Students can register their vehicles, obtain parking information, and pick up parking permits at a parking service drive-through.

Identifying effective communication techniques to inform adults of available student services is critical. Adult students may not read the campus paper, see the posters or flyers in the student union, or listen to youth-oriented radio stations. Therefore, information about services and activities needs to be delivered to adult students in ways that are likely to reach them. Newsletters periodically sent directly to adults at home can effectively highlight student service programs, adult-oriented campus events or programs, and adult student accomplishments while promoting a sense of community.

Other institutions rely on less traditional methods to reach adult learners. The Office of Adult Learner and Commuter Student Programs at Iowa State University in Ames, Iowa, sends all new adult students paper lunch bags filled with coupons and information about programs and services available at the university. Approximately a week before the start of each semester, program personnel mail a welcome letter to students that introduces the brown bag theme. Trying an on-line approach, the Student Assistance Center at the University of Akron (Akron, Ohio) created two on-line information programs, "Ask Aunt Phoebe" and "Ask an Advisor," to reach adult learners. Both are available on the Internet 24 hours a day. Students can ask "Aunt

Phoebe" anything—questions about policies and procedures, student services, or even relationship issues. "Ask an Advisor" is a forum for addressing specific advising issues. Students receive feedback immediately by e-mail.

Many campuses have adult student centers or one-stop centers that provide information on student services programs. The next section provides more details on these centers. For centers to be effective, adults must be aware of their existence. At Kansas State University (Manhattan, Kansas), the adult student center has devised an eye-catching, distinctive logo. Logo-imprinted posters placed at numerous sites on campus provide information on all of the agency's services as well as its location and hours of operation. These remind adult students of services available at the center and provide visibility for adults on campus.

In summary, the context of adult learners' lives should dictate techniques to inform adults about student services and on-campus activities. The reality is that adults may spend little or no time on campus. Strategies that involve how to provide accessible services and how to publicize important information will vary from campus to campus; the strategy that works for an urban community college will not necessarily work for a large land grant institution in a rural setting. To develop a strategy, institutions need a clear picture of who their adult students are demographically. If, for example, the majority of entering adults are low-income students, and have limited access to computers, technology-based methods will be ineffective. Assuring that student services are accessible to adult learners require that institutions have a clear idea of who their adult learners are and when and how those learners are most likely to use and learn about services. Only then can a comprehensive plan be developed for that institution.

If services are inaccessible to adults or if adults are unaware of services' existence, adults are shortchanged. Further, if services are designed for younger students without considering the special needs of adult students their needs will go unmet. It would be neither realistic nor wise to recommend that two separate students service systems be established—one for traditional-aged students and one for older students. A successful response to the challenge posed by the unique circumstances of the older student generally requires an expansion of existing services. Such an expansion occurs most dependably when adult student advocates are able to increase the visibility of these students by making service providers aware of their needs and circumstances. Readers who want to encourage their institution to broaden its efforts to serve adult learners may want to consider some suggested advocacy activities discussed in Chapter 7.

Some institutions have found that they can enhance their success in responding to the needs of older students by establishing one additional service. In its simplest form it is commonly referred to as the "One Stop Informational Center"; in its more comprehensive form, it is known as the "Adult Student Center." The organization of these centers and the services they provide vary widely from campus to campus depending on institutional needs and priorities.

Both one-stop information centers and adult service centers serve as locations where adults go to find information and referral to other student service agencies on campus. Because adults rarely reside on campus, they often speak of having no home on campus and no place to leave their things; they often describe themselves as nomadic "bag people." For many older students, these centers become their home away from home and help alleviate their feelings of marginality. Although many younger commuter students may face similar situations, they may have residential friends to socialize with, or they may feel more comfortable than adults with carrying backpacks and spending time in the union or other youth-oriented campus locations.

One-Stop Informational and Adult Student Center Functions

At a minimum, these centers should have up-to-date information on all student services on campus. Some examples of the types of information that might be provided are as follows:

Financial Aid. Types of aid along with eligibility requirements and application deadlines should be available in a resource book as well as on-line. Assistance in the application process should be available.

Counseling Services. Available counseling resources on campus and in the community should be listed, along with the specialized services they provide (for example, stress reduction and time management information). The appointment process and fee policies should be detailed.

Academic and Learning Assistance. Campuses vary widely in terms of who provides academic assistance. The learning center should inform adults about sources of assistance (such as the writing assistance center and computer skills labs) and provide tutoring lists or services. Additionally, the center should publicize workshops that focus on common concerns of adult students (for example, study and test-taking skills).

Child Care Services. On-campus child care options and their hours, eligibility requirements, and other information should be available. Because many parents prefer to arrange for child care in their neighborhoods, providing lists of community child care resources can also be helpful. Additionally, many institutions have initiated an emergency number locator service so that adults can be easily located while on campus. This can be critical to easing the worry of parents who leave their children with campus- or community-based childcare.

Campus Activities. Adult students are often uninformed about after-class educational opportunities due to the fact that they spend little or no time on campus. They are more likely to attend lectures, films, and other special campus activities if they are made aware of these opportunities.

On some campuses, centers have evolved from being informational centers to becoming the social center for adult students. Such centers provide informal places for adults to exchange views and develop friendships with other students. Having a designated place for such gatherings can create a sense of community. Center staff can assist this process in various ways (for example, by organizing brown bag lunches or dinners where students invite a favorite professor, or where a professor addresses a topic of interest such as women's nutritional needs). Centers can also sponsor informal sessions where adult students can be introduced to student support staff. There are numerous ways centers can help adult students connect with each other, faculty, and the greater campus.

It may also be important for some adult students to discover ways to connect their family members to their campus experience. Families that have been included in campus activities and introduced to the demands placed on college students may be more likely to provide the kind of support that contributes to success. Involving family members in on-campus activities can help them understand where their family member is when "at school." The adult learner center can become the ideal agency to organize family days or activities on campus. Soliciting free tickets for on campus movies or for sporting events can be helpful to the families of students who may not have much money for entertainment.

As noted in Chapter 7, an adult center's staff can serve as advocates for new programs and increase awareness of adult student needs. Sometimes faculty and student service personnel are unaware of the number of adults on campus or the unique educational challenges they confront as students. Raising the visibility of adults on campus and serving as the voice of the adult in the student service community is an important function of a comprehensive center.

All adult learner centers will not and should not look alike; they should reflect the needs and nature of their unique populations as well as the circumstances of the institution. Most centers will provide informational and referral services. In those colleges where significant populations of adults are on campus, a center has the potential to do much more. It can serve as a community-building organization for adult students as well as an agency that informs other student service agencies about the special needs of adult learners.

An Example

Emporia State University's Nontraditional Center (Emporia, Kansas) models the ways a center can serve adults. Located in its own facility, the center provides a campus home for adult students. Because the university offers few evening or weekend classes the center is open throughout the day. Equipped with tables and chairs, refrigerators, and a microwave, the center provides students a place to eat and mingle with other adult students. Comfortable couches and chairs create areas where students can relax before, between, and after class, and they offer a quiet place for study. Lockers are available to store books or other belongings. The building has a playroom for students' children when their parents are using the center's facilities. Computers are available for student use, and for those unfamiliar with computers, help is provided. The center serves as a one-stop shop for preenrollment and for various items of information such as housing, child care, and financial aid. A paid peer counselor is on staff to serve as an advocate and problem solver.

An active adult student organization at Emporia State University's Nontraditional Center organizes participation in community service and raises money for nontraditional student scholarships. The Single Parent Advocate Resource Connection matches volunteers on campus with single parents on campus or single parents in the local community. A single-parent support group meets with programs that alternate between invited speakers and activities with participant's children. Other social activities open to all adult students include a welcome potluck, a holiday gathering, and a spring reception that honors scholarship recipients.

The center's director reports to the vice president for student affairs and sits on numerous campus committees, including orientation, diversity education, alcohol and drug abuse, transfer students, and child development. By participating in committee meetings, the director communicates the needs of the adult student to the greater campus community and ensures that the voice of each student is heard.

Agencies within a university or college that hold primary responsibility for adult students can be structured in a variety of ways. The focus of the agency—creating community, promoting campus involvement, disseminating information, or serving as an advocate for the adult learner on campus—will dictate the way in which the organization is structured.

We turn now to select areas of student affairs that are of

special relevance to adult students. Each of those areas will be examined and principles of good practice delineated.

Orientation

Orientation is one of the first opportunities the campus has to identify the adult students' needs and to provide assistance. It is vital that adults receive immediate orientation and advisement. This is especially important for those who enter with concerns about their ability to succeed. Many adult students speak of feeling disconnected and isolated initially, unsure or unaware of where to go for assistance. Orientation programs that focus on issues of interest to younger students will not adequately address the concerns of adult students.

Schlossberg, Lynch, and Chickering (1989) suggest that initial orientations for adults should both present information and provide opportunities for adult learners to interact with faculty, staff, and other adult learners. Intensive orientations assist adults with identifying campus resources and provide students the opportunity to ask questions and begin to feel as though they are part of campus life.

Adults are often tightly bound by work schedules and may be unable to attend a scheduled orientation program. Programs presented on a variety of dates and times are more likely to be accessible to adults. The American Council on Education's (ACE) *Focus on Adults* (2001) suggests that orientation programs for adults be multimedia and presented at a variety of times. For those unable to attend such sessions, supplementary resources should be available. Examples of multimedia orientation supplements include videotapes, Web pages, brochures, or resource guides.

ACE also stresses the importance of a handbook containing all relevant information. Ohio University (Athens, Ohio) provides the *Resources Guide,* a detailed explanation of the student services office and its hours of operation, as a means to inform new students of campus resources. A quarterly newsletter follows with information on university and community events.

Orientation is an ongoing process. As adults progress through the school year, new questions and issues surface that were not initially apparent. Difficulties with stress or relationships may appear later in the semester, and information presented at a one-time orientation at the beginning of the school year may not be recalled.

Some campuses offer an intensive, ongoing orientation course throughout the term. This format provides opportunities for adults to explore topics such as learning styles, study skills, and life and vocational plans. Because adult students are heterogeneous, designing smaller orientation programs for certain subgroups may be the best way to serve the unique needs of some adult learners. For example, the University of Massachusetts — Boston's Veterans Upward Bound Program involves a 14-week preenrollment course designed to encourage and prepare military veterans to enroll in college courses. The program recognizes the need for confidence building and skills remediation. Described as a tough academic boot camp, it offers counseling. Reentry women, first generation students, and minority populations are other examples of subgroups that might benefit from orientations geared toward their unique characteristics. Those designing semester-long orientation programs must consider several issues: what to include in the course, whether credit will be offered for the course, or if credit given for the course would be transferable to other institutions.

The ACE *Focus on Adults* (2001) publication suggests the following as topics to cover in a credit course: learning styles, academic preparedness, study skills, achievement levels, available campus resources, and coping with transitions. Additional issues to include in credit or noncredit orientations include evaluating prior experience and determining its relationship to educational goals; exploring professional, vocational, and life-cycle plans and aspirations; reviewing academic program alternatives and requirements that affect adult learners; and analyzing time commitments and competing responsibilities.

Orientation sessions that include family members or are designed for family members are beneficial in generating support for the adult student at home. Some institutions include in their orientation programs a panel discussion involving spouses of currently enrolled students. The panel can prepare spouses for changes that might be needed or created by their partner's return to school, and it can also serve to validate the feelings a partner may be experiencing. Other institutions have offered orientation programs at times when children can be brought to campus. For example, separate children's activities agenda can be planned to coincide with the adult student's orientation program.

Those responsible for orientation programs on campus need to monitor these programs to ensure that the needs of adult learners are being considered and met. Such monitoring should include checks on the convenience of program times, the relevance of content, the provisions for ongoing orientation, and the availability of alternatives to face-to-face attendance.

Orientation programs often identify one area of immediate interest to many adult students—academic and learning assistance.

Academic and Learning Assistance Support

Many adult learners come to campus fearful of their ability to succeed in the classroom. Some have experienced failure in the past and have been told that they weren't college material. It has been years since most adult students engaged in any type of formal schooling. They are concerned that they won't remember how to study, how to write an essay, or how to take a test. Instructors, whether student service providers, or departmental personnel, must be sensitive to the special vulnerability of adult students. Brushing off or ignoring adult learners concerns and becoming impatient with the adult learner's persistent need for reassurance may lead to an adult student's withdrawal from campus.

The connection with campus resources needs to be made quickly before these adults lose confidence in their ability to succeed or before they fall behind academically. As discussed previously, knowing what services are available, how to access them and being able to use them at convenient times and in a comfortable mode will be imperative. Campuses vary widely in how and where they provide academic support. Academic departments may be solely responsible for learning assistance. On other campuses, learning centers provide assistance in developing basic writing, math, and computer skills. Tutoring may be available from a variety of on-campus sources, including academic departments, student organizations and adult learning centers. Adults differ from younger students in how quickly they can process new information; therefore, a fast-paced, complex class is likely to be more difficult for an adult. Integrating the realities of prior experience and knowledge with academic learning from the "Ivory Tower" can also be a difficult process. If those providing learning assistance are not aware of these characteristics of adult learners, they may be ineffective in providing help. Peer assistance programs can be especially beneficial to adults as they face returning to an academic environment. Recently returned adults who have successfully navigated academic waters are more likely to understand adult concerns and build confidence than are younger peers.

For those who speak English as a second language (ESL), an additional layer of difficulty is added. Arrangements need to be made to ensure that the learning needs of this group of adult students are met. If the campus does not have an ESL program that can assist these students, a listing of community based programs should be made available.

Although both adult and younger students may seek out the same assistance programs, their different needs may make some programs more crucial for one group than another. Many majors require at least one basic math course; certain careers are closed to those unable to negotiate this hurdle. But more than any other discipline, mathematics can strike fear in the heart of returning adults. This is especially true for women who grew up in an era when mathematical competence was considered unnecessary. Although institutions commonly provide math labs to assist students with poor math skills, they may not recognize the impact of adult student anxiety. One-on-one attention from tutors trained to work specifically with adults often becomes necessary. Especially helpful are mature tutors who understand the needs of the adult student and the impact each student's anxiety and self-doubts can have on their performance. Effective tutors assist in skill development, but they can also help build learner confidence.

Writing in the work world is quite different from academic writing. Term papers and essays can seem formidable to someone who is accustomed to writing nothing more complex than memos. Mrs. Jones's senior English class may seem far removed, and demands for organizing thoughts and expressing them correctly can be daunting. Many institutions have writing labs that can be of assistance to the adult learner. Personnel in the lab, however, should be sensitized to the embarrassment created by an adult student's inability to write well. Sensitivity can go a long way toward encouraging the adult to seek additional help and to persist in school.

Many adults enter college more comfortable with the now-defunct card catalog than with the computer when its capabilities and operation are unknown. They will need instruction in using the technology resources available to help them conduct library searches. Learning how to get access to the information available through different databases will be critical to their success. Although some libraries do offer excellent orientation programs, their staffs also need to consider offering an in-depth examination of technology's potential for those who have little experience and who consider themselves "dummies" when it comes to computers. Such a program would help adults make full use of new information resources. Library personnel responsible for facilitating orientation programs must keep in mind that many adults may be reluctant to admit their inability to use computer-based resources. Understanding the adult learner's anxiety is the first step in increasing her or his willingness and ability to use these resources in the future.

When providing academic and learning assistance support for adults, specialists need to consider each student's confidence level, learning and processing speeds, and language facility. Several different methods can be used to deliver assistance: workshops, individual counseling sessions, computerized assistance, content area tutoring, and academic support groups. A variety of formats and hours need to be available so adults can have access to these services based on their preferences and other demands. Those who staff these assistance programs should be aware of adult issues and learning characteristics since they may make the difference between success and failure in the classroom.

Academic and learning assistance services are clearly linked to retention (Casazza & Silverman, 1996). Adults who feel they are unable to learn and are therefore wasting valuable family resources to attend college are at high risk for dropping out. Services that strengthen both their confidence and their skills clearly promote persistence and success.

Career Counseling Center

Adult learners most often cite career-related concerns as the reason for their entry into higher education. Whether by helping them to advance in a current position or to change careers, adults commonly expect the college experience to influence their careers in positive ways. Many adults enter college with clear goals related to their current career. Yet to assume adults have specific career goals and accurate career information is a mistake. In a national study of career counselors at public community colleges, the most frequently reported student career problem was "lack of career goals" (65.5%), described as career indecision and lack of knowledge about self in relations to careers (Coll, 1995). Because adults represent a large proportion of those enrolled at community colleges, this high percentage sends a clear signal to those who work with them. Many adults lack accurate and up-to-date information about career qualifications, employment opportunities, or how experience and abilities mesh with career opportunities. Therefore, career-counseling staffs need to work with adult students in a multifaceted manner and focus on several issues.

Initially, it is important to evaluate the support needs of adult students. As noted in earlier chapters, many adults enter college as part of a life transition. Counselors need to understand how these transitions affect and influence beliefs and attitudes about career issues. An adult who returns because of job loss may first need reassurance about his or her abilities, whereas an adult who is returning to qualify for promotion in their current field may need information about career requirements for advancement.

Providing support and determining the level of knowledge adults have about careers, career decision making, and their career information needs are important initial functions of career counseling. Developing a realistic career plan early in their academic career is imperative to many adults, especially those plagued by financial difficulties who do not have the time or financial resources to engage in false starts.

Career counselors can assist adults in developing career life goals. Career life planning involves a variety of factors that influence career choice, including values, abilities, interests, and work-life experiences. Several conceptual frameworks and evaluation tools can help to facilitate the process of developing a career life plan.

Hansen's Integrative Life Planning (ILP) model is an excellent conceptual framework for use with adults because it focuses on how to integrate values, abilities, and experience as an aid to setting priorities. *Integrative Life Planning: Critical Tasks for Career Development and Changing Life Patterns* (Hansen, 1997) explains the tenets of ILP and offers practical suggestions on how to conduct workshops based on its principles. Workshops can include a variety of self-awareness activities designed to assist individuals in making thoughtful life decisions. Adults become more complex and heterogeneous as they age; ILP is a paradigm that acknowledges and supports this complexity.

Another conceptual framework that reflects the complexity of career decision making in adulthood is the life-career rainbow concept presented by Super (1990). Super's definition of career acknowledges the multiple roles that adults assume, including work, family, and leisure. This expanded view of career may be useful to adults who are acquiring the role of student. It provides the opportunity to examine the implications of their new role: What does it mean to be a student? How much time will be invested in the student aspect of their life? How will the student make adjustments in her or his life based on the new demands of being a student?

Super acknowledges the influence multiple roles and life cycle stage have on career development. Self-knowledge and knowledge of the career being considered are viewed as key elements in making a wise career decision. Exploration from multiple perspectives (learning styles, locus of control, self-efficacy) is more useful than focusing on single characteristics. Because Super incorporates multiple theories and attempts to explain how personality, abilities, needs, values, interests, and self-concept interact to determine an appropriate career choice, it is an excellent framework to use when planning career counseling activities for adults.

Two instruments are especially useful in this exploratory process, the learning styles inventory (LSI) (Kolb, 1984) and the self-directed search (SDS) (Holland, 1997). The LSI identifies the student's preferred learning style and the academic majors and career areas that are compatiable to this style. It's an excellent way to examine prior learning and work experience as they relate to career plans. The SDS is based on the assumption that occupational choice is influenced by personality. Holland (1997) has shown that members of certain occupational groups have similar personalities; for occupational success and satisfaction, there needs to be congruence between the individual's personality and the job environment. Career counselors can also convert adults' leisure interests and previous successful work experience into Holland codes, thus providing other occupational areas to explore. Therefore, the self-directed search can be used as an instrument that directs adults to occupational areas where they are likely to be successful.

Isaacson and Brown (2000) describe two computerized systems that can be used for further career exploration. *SIGI PLUS* is a computerized system that asks adult students to respond to questions and then provides immediate personalized feedback. Local resources and information are included and updated so that material of special interest to adults who may want to change jobs but wish to stay in the local community remains relevant.

The Discover II system combines information about the world of work, the student, and occupational choices. A special feature relevant to adult students is the inclusion of a module on making transitions.

Not all institutions can afford computerized systems; and even if these are available, they do not meet all of the needs of adult students. Career counseling personnel need to administer relevant instruments, provide one-on-one counseling, gather information about job trends and local job opportunities relevant to adults. Counseling services need to be available at times and places accessible to older learners.

Setting priorities in services, determining staffing capabilities, and examining how current staff can provide services become necessary responsibilities of the service provider. If adult students are to receive appropriate assistance, a number of questions must be answered: What information can be conveyed via pamphlets, newsletters on-line, and in periodically scheduled workshops? How can exploratory instruments be administered at a variety of times and in a variety of locations? Which workshop topics are most relevant to adults?

Workshops are ideal formats for introducing adult learners to Hansen's and Super's conceptual frameworks. Offering workshops relating to coping skills for adults in transition and resume' writing, with a focus on transferable skills, are additional ways to respond to the needs of returning adult students. A community-based career workshop is an outreach activity that could attract off-campus adults and increase enrollment. Many adults need access to career information before deciding to enroll.

As stated earlier, most adults are not interested in spending their time or money on educational programs that provide no improvement in their employment situation. At the most basic level, adults need help in answering these questions: Who am I? What can I do? What do I like to do? What careers will allow me to use my preferred skills to make a decent living? What careers are available locally? Because adults come in more varied shapes and sizes and carrying heavier baggage than younger students, simplistic solutions to their complex career issues are inappropriate.

Personal Counseling

In addition to the many transitions discussed earlier, education may cause adults to question beliefs and attitudes, transforming them in the process and affecting their personal relationships with family and friends. During such a period of turbulence, many adults could profit from personal counseling. Schlossberg, Lynch, and Chickering (1989) note that adults will bring multiple counseling needs to the campus. Although therapeutic intervention may sometimes be required, they believe that counselors should emphasize a proactive prevention orientation, helping adult learners build on strengths and identifying or establishing personal support systems.

Adults bring different counseling issues to the campus than do younger students. Developing support groups that connect adults with others in similar circumstances is often a function of mental health professionals. Single parents, the recently divorced or widowed, those who have recently lost jobs due to downsizing, reentry women, and retirees are all populations that might find group support beneficial. Problems with establishing support groups may be adults' time constraints, reluctance to seek counseling on campus, and a lack of awareness by the counseling staff of adults' needs. If adults are rarely on campus, mental health staffs are unlikely to encounter them and may assume adults are not interested in support group opportunities. Evening and weekend off-campus workshops or programs focused on adult counseling needs may help mental health staff connect with those in need of specific types of support groups.

Programs that meet the mental health needs of adults include marital counseling, parenting techniques, assistance with mid-life issues, alcohol and drug abuse prevention, and stress management. Wellness programs that address stress reduction, coping skills, and relaxation techniques can short-circuit poor health, anxiety, and depression. Workshops that address time management, goal-setting, and specific transitions—such as losing one's spouse, regrouping after losing one's job, or becoming an empty nester—are especially appropriate for adults.

Counseling or mental health center staff may find it impossible to offer the multitude of workshops needed to meet the needs of a diverse campus population. There may be other programs on campus that could assist in sponsoring workshops and seminars geared toward adult learner concerns. For example, some campuses have graduate programs in marriage and family counseling or in nutrition and exercise physiology. Faculty members or advanced graduate students from these programs may be good resources. Additionally, off-campus agencies might offer program assistance. This, of course, requires having a good relationship with community resources and knowing reputable individuals who might be willing to offer occasional workshops designed for adult students.

Counseling centers need to explore alternative ways in which counseling needs might be met. Brochures, videos, books, Web sites, chat room support groups, and programs on local campus television stations are examples of ways adult students could be reached. Mental health and counseling professionals can be key players in providing support to adult students at an often-stressful period in their lives. By developing proactive, aggressive programs to assist adults, they could make the difference between success and failure.

Involving Adults in On-Campus Organizations

Participation in student organizations has been shown to be beneficial in promoting identification with the institution and in developing interpersonal, leadership, and managerial skills. Although not all adults will choose to be active in on-campus groups, encouragement to become more involved and activities related to their interests might increase their attendance. Some adults may be interested in participating in organizations made especially for other adults. Many campuses have adult student organizations that sponsor programs geared toward the interests of the adult students. Offerings that include significant others and family members are especially effective.

Adult student groups often have unstable histories, vacillating from large active memberships to small inactive memberships. Student affairs personnel who advise adult student groups should understand that as adults move out of the group and new members move in, a shift in interests and circumstances is likely to occur. Success should not be measured by numbers in the group but by how well the group meets the needs of those who do choose to participate. The focus for the student affairs specialist should be on facilitating—assisting those interested in participating in planning activities and programs and in advertising the group's existence.

Because adult learners do not participate as actively on campus as younger students do, fewer opportunities exist for them to be recognized for their achievement. There are several national honor societies, however, that recognize academic and leadership accomplishments by adults specifically, including the Pinnacle, the Alpha Omega Honor Society, and Alpha Sigma Lambda. These organizations are often highly selective, requiring participation in campus or community activities, or both, and a demonstration of leadership. By including community participation as well as on-campus participation, these organizations acknowledge that service can take place both on and off campus.

Alpha Sigma Lambda has the most stringent academic requirements; members must be in the top 10% of their class and have a minimum grade point average of 3.2 (B+). One of the purposes of this society is to build community among adult students. Illustrative activities include the following:

Simpson College (Indianola, Iowa) sponsors family-oriented activities such as a family pizza party and family swim party.
La Salle University (Philadelphia, Pennsylvania) provides a tutoring service for adult students and presents a seminar each semester on "Successful Study Techniques."
Kean College of New Jersey (Union, New Jersey) sponsors an induction dinner in the fall where a memorial scholarship is presented to a society

member in recognition of both academic merit and community service. A "Teacher-of-the-Year" award is presented to a faculty member.

IN SUMMARY

Although adult students' needs may be similar in some ways to those of younger students, adult students bring many unique needs and concerns to campus. These needs challenge those involved with student services to examine and evaluate their practices to ensure that they are responsive to adult student situations. Understanding who the adult student is on a particular campus is the first step in planning appropriate services. An institutional emphasis on older learners is needed to enhance the provision of responsive student service programs. It is beneficial if there is one agency on campus, such as an adult learner center, that serves adult students. When this is not possible, having at least one person per student service agency responsible for representing the voice of adult learners can be effective. Even then, the adult learner can fall through the cracks. Finally, student affairs personnel need to be aware that the adult student population is not only heterogeneous but also constantly changing. Therefore, needs assessment for this population should be an ongoing, dynamic process.

CHAPTER 7

Solidifying Campus Support through Advocacy

Our goal is to provide an environment in which adult students can build confidence in their abilities, gain clarity in their educational goals, and develop a strategy for attaining those goals. This is facilitated by a close working relationship with faculty, an opportunity to develop peer support, and an open door to information and counseling provided by program staff members. An additional goal is increasing awareness of the university community of adults and their different needs. —Goal statement for an Adult Learning Center

Personally, I disagree with the whole concept of nontraditional programs for adults. Barriers to traditional degree pursuit affect all students. Going to college is a major commitment to one's life. It changes timetables, delays things, and requires some sacrifices. The student truly wanting a degree will gladly accept the inconvenience and sacrifice. I am not sure we want any other kind. —Faculty member of a major university

Each of these quotes provides a persuasive argument for advocacy on behalf of adult learners in higher education. The first quote represents the goal statement of an award-winning adult learner program. This program includes a director, an assistant director, a counselor, a secretary, and three student assistants. Effective advocacy efforts may have contributed to this program's expansion and continuation even after a change in university administration. Reflected in the second quote is an attitude steeped in the traditional view that higher education requires full-time, residential attendance. This quote illustrates how much advocacy work needs to be done if faculty, administrators, and student service providers are to respond effectively to adult learners.

Because each institution is unique in its setting, history, mission, facilities, curricula, administrators, faculty, and students, no single plan can be advanced to enhance the campus experience of adult students. What is universally true is that merely adding services and programs designed specifically for adult students to already existing campus offerings does not adequately ensure an appropriate level of campus understanding and support.

The importance of having a designated advocate, ombudsman, or office for a new student group has been affirmed through experience with international, minority, and disabled students. The presence of similar advocates could be equally important for adult learners. Many institutional leaders, however, are not prepared to invest the personnel and financial resources that formal advocacy mechanisms require. Therefore, those who work for and with adult students may need to assume the role of advocate on a volunteer, pro bono basis.

No matter how effectively some needs of individual adult students are served, assuring fair and equitable treatment from all aspects of the institution remains a critical goal. Adult learner advocates can be pivotal to reaching this goal because they raise important questions, encourage others to examine critical issues, and facilitate changes needed to increase institution-wide responsiveness to adult learners.

ADVOCACY—WHAT IS IT?

The purpose of advocacy is to ensure that adult learners are represented, recognized, and integrated into institution-wide planning. The process of advocacy has both formal and informal dimensions; effective advocates use both to accomplish their goals. Formal advocacy works within an institution's organizational structure through such activities as submitting proposals or recommending modifications in programs and services. Informal advocacy involves behind-the-scenes activities, such as volunteering to serve on important campus committees that lay the groundwork for formal advocacy by increasing awareness of and sensitivity to the concerns of adult learners.

In pursuing their main purpose, advocates address three goals. First, they seek to create an awareness of adult learner characteristics and needs. They do this by involving themselves in a variety of campus activities where these differences can be communicated—admissions committees, orientation committees, student retention committees, and, if possible, administrative boards such as the administrative council.

A second goal of advocacy is to provide a voice for adult learners that clearly articulates how their needs and learning experiences are distinct from those of traditional students. Examples of creative advocacy efforts that pursue this goal include sponsoring an adult learner awareness week and sponsoring a monthly dean's forum where adults can express their concerns and frustrations directly to those who can take appropriate action.

Finally, advocacy seeks to encourage and influence the modification of attitudes, policies, and programs so that they will better serve this diverse student group. Understanding how learners have experienced the campus environment can be central to achieving this final advocacy goal. Such information can identify the institutional barriers that impede success and provide concrete suggestions for modifications.

This chapter will examine each of these three goals and suggest ways advocates can be instrumental in addressing them.

ADVOCACY—CREATING AWARENESS

Many challenges that adult learners confront in higher education are unintended consequences of systems initially designed to serve full-time, resident students. A critical component of effective advocacy is uncovering the sometimes subtle connections an institutional community has to the mindset created by this emphasis on traditional-aged learners. A close examination of an institution's facilities, programs, services, policies, and publications will dramatically expose the extent to which the campus has been structured almost exclusively for traditional students.

Gathering information about the adult learners' experiences within the institution is critical to initiating institutional changes; it will be addressed later in this chapter. Advocacy efforts designed to sensitize the campus community to adult learners rely on less formal methods of data collection. Advocacy at this level requires simple, basic, demographic information about adult learners and their enrollment patterns. Such data are usually available from the assessment office or registrar.

The information that can successfully create awareness is generally easy to obtain: What proportion of the current student body consists of learners over age 25? How many of these are enrolled on a part-time basis? What is their average credit load? What percentage takes courses during the evening? How many are new to the institution? How many are returning students? How many are non-degree-seeking? To what degree do they rely on financial aid?

Some potentially useful information may be more troublesome to gather than the above data: What distance do adult learners live from the campus? What is their typical travel time to and from campus? How much time do they spend on campus? What are their short- and long-range goals? What are their family responsibilities?

Administrators, faculty, program directors, and staff can relate to "numbers." Answering questions like those just posed can be instrumental in shifting interests in the direction of becoming a more inclusive campus that strives for equity in programs, services, and the allocation of resources. Presenting this demographic information and its programmatic implications to prominent campus decision-makers becomes a key advocacy task. A direct approach usually means involvement in institutional committees. It may have to be done indirectly, however, by priming "connected" individuals, who then carry the message to influential decision-makers.

This approach may be the only choice available to advocates who work outside the mainstream of student services programming. Some advocates, due to their campus assignment, are isolated and may need to utilize this indirect approach to influence institutional change.

Dealing with simple issues, such as a student's inability to attend a required orientation meeting due to work conflicts, may merely involve taking the opportunity to meet campus service providers and discussing individual cases with them directly. Many advocacy efforts, however, involve changing an institution-wide policy requiring multiple levels of administrative agreement. Changes of this magnitude are usually initiated by a committee, and an advocate's involvement can become critical.

Sometimes volunteering to serve is enough to get one appointed to an influential committee. It is more difficult to get appointed to committees with high institutional status and power (such as the administrative council). Representatives from large, visible programs often have direct access to higher administrative councils and committees. But individuals who represent a small unit with limited visibility will seldom be appointed to such committees unless they are assertive. This may require seeking advice from administrators to whom one's unit reports as to how one gets appointed to such committees. Such inquiries will be more effective if the advocate can provide relevant data (collected through some of the means discussed later in this chapter) and can offer a persuasive rationale for why the advocate's committee membership is vital to the institution and its adult learners.

Important committees in which to seek involvement include the admissions committee, financial aid and scholarship committee, student retention committee, and any other committee whose policies and decisions affect adult students directly. Members of these committees often lack an understanding of the impact their policy decisions have on this segment of the student population. For example, adult learners with interrupted attendance records and low rates of progress are often ignored by policies related to financial aid, admission status, course sequences, and service eligibilities (for example, library use, computer-center access, and tutoring). Adults who want to move through the system rapidly by carrying unusually heavy loads and attending year-round may discover that policies designed for traditional students are insensitive to their circumstances. For example, grants, scholarships, and fellowships are often limited to those who follow more traditional enrollment patterns.

Advocates should also be involved in committees that make fee schedule recommendations. It is often up to the advocate to pose such awkward questions as the following: "Do adult learners receive the services for which they pay (for example, campus activities)?" "Is the revenue received from adult learners spent in ways that benefit them?" By raising these questions, adult learner advocates can be pivotal in developing policies that are equitable for all students.

Another area in which advocate involvement may be useful involves technology-based degree programs. Although technology may increase the learning options available to adults, it can also increase learner isolation. Too often virtual learners have been viewed exclusively as enrollment builders; little consideration has been given to how technology-based processes affect other aspects of college attendance. Advocates must concentrate energy on guaranteeing that the needs of adult learners in distance-based programs get addressed as effectively as those of campus-based learners. Gaining an appointment to the distance education committee is a good way to become influential in this arena.

These examples have shown how committee involvement can help create institutional awareness of adult learners' needs and characteristics. Creating an adult learner advisory board can also impact institutional awareness. Although it is crucial to have advisory group representatives who are sensitive to adult learner concerns and committed to enhancing the campus experience for this student population, it is also desirable to appoint members with high visibility who are *not* aware of the special nature of adult learner needs. Through advisory board involvement, these leaders often become more interested and informed; ultimately, some serve as adult learner advocates.

In addition to including currently enrolled adult learners and university-based representatives on an advisory board, individuals from the community should be asked to serve. Prominent community leaders who are alumni and who completed their degree work as adults could be valuable committee members. Such individuals frequently share personal insights that can lead to concrete suggestions for more effectively serving adult learners.

Community representatives from the Chamber of Commerce, local employers who provide tuition assistance, and others who promise to add prestige and power to the committee can be helpful not only in developing strategies for creating institutional change but also in indirectly influencing key campus administrators. A by-product of their membership may be increased scholarship funds and donations to help host adult-learner campus activities.

Readers who seek insights and suggestions as to the establishment and functioning of advisory boards might find Kowalski's (1988) book on *The Organization and Planning of Adult Education* very helpful. Kowalski's outline of the critical steps to board formation is particularly valuable.

Soliciting the support of other units on campus might be an additional strategy for advocates to explore. For example, some advocates may find their campus Division of Continuing Education to be an important source of support. Although organized very differently from one campus to another, a common concern is serving adult learners. While the effectiveness with which such units impact institutional change can be as varied as their organizational structures, they can be powerful allies for adult student advocates and important to creating a campus awareness about adult learners. Individuals seeking to modify their campus community for older students must identify multiple sources of influence and support. A close examination of the various units across ones' institution can help expose potential advocates.

Finally, individuals who are committed to consciousness-raising efforts will solicit the assistance of currently enrolled adult learners. Some campuses have adult learner organizations that serve as a logical source for student advocacy. Given the proper leadership from advocates, these organizations can provide the impetus for institutional change. If such organizations are not in place, advocates can assist adult learners with exploring the steps for creating one, including conducting a needs assessment for determining if such an organization would be viable.

An alternative to developing a formal organization is to encourage individual learners with leadership qualities to participate in campus organizations. Being represented in student government, programming councils, and other critical decision-making bodies will ensure awareness of an adult learner's perspective. Adult learners can exert considerable pressure for change through involvement on program and policy committees. Finding an adult learner who is willing to commit the time such activities demand poses a special challenge to the advocate.

Off-campus based students are frequently overlooked. In the past, such adult learners were excluded from membership on campus committees simply by their geographical isolation. Technological advances make it possible for them to be involved in ways that were previously unavailable. Advocates can call attention to opportunities for using technology to expand student representativeness.

Adult learners also have important linkages to communities. Some may already occupy leadership positions within the community. Even if they don't have "clout" of their own, they often know and can influence someone who does. Community leaders are frequently influential with institutional administrators because of their perpetual concern with town-and-gown issues and with public relations. Identifying students with these linkages and soliciting their assistance represents an additional advocacy strategy.

Heightening an institution's awareness of adult learner concerns is an essential goal. There are no universal solutions for how it can best be addressed. Adult learner advocates should explore all of the ideas just presented and seek additional options that their unique situations may require.

PROVIDING A VOICE TO ADULT STUDENTS

Some institutions empower adult learners to communicate their needs and unique concerns to the campus community. This not only allows the learner to help take responsibility for initiating change but it also communicates to adults that their voice matters.

Mattering is a concept originally labeled by Rosenberg (Rosenberg & McCullough, 1981) and later applied to work with adult learners in higher education by Schlossberg (Schlossberg, Lassalle, & Golec, 1989). It refers to the beliefs (right or wrong) that people have about how much they matter to someone else and to what extent someone's attention focuses on them. Mattering also involves people's beliefs about how much others care about and appreciate them. This concept was the basis for a useful psychometric device, "The Mattering Scales for Adult Students in Higher Education" (Schlossberg et al., 1989). Results from this instrument help institutions discover adult learners' perceptions of how well an institution has responded to their needs and where those needs are met. The results also indicate the areas where adult learners perceive deficiencies in the institution's services.

Unlike some of the data collection methods discussed later in this chapter, this research tool is not designed to measure how satisfied adults are with the institution's response to their needs. Instead, it examines the general perceptions that adult students have of the higher education environment. The instrument can be administered to groups or individuals and involves less than 20 minutes. It includes five subscales:

1. Administrative—to assess perceptions of how sensitive campus policies and procedures are to adult student concerns;

2. Advising—to assess perceptions of advisors' and other information providers' attentiveness;

3. Peer—to assess perceptions of belongingness and peer acceptance;

4. Multiple roles—to assess perceptions of how well the campus recognizes competing demands on a learner's time; and

5. Faculty—to assess perceptions of the extent to which faculty members treat learners equitably and capitalize on the educational value of their life experiences.

Data gathered from this instrument can be used to pinpoint areas in which adult learners feel they do not matter, a first step toward taking action to create a more hospitable environment. This instrument can be purchased from the American Council on Education. It is also included in their publication, *Focus on Adults* (2001), which is described in depth later.

Some useful alternative ideas about how to collect related information can be found in the resource, *Serving Commuter Students: Examples of Good Practice* (National Clearinghouse for Commuter Programs, 1998, 1993). One such example is the "Annual Fireside Chat" sponsored by the University of Toledo's president (Toledo, Ohio). Adult students are invited to attend a dinner during which they are encouraged to discuss any aspect of adult student life. From a random mailing to 500 such students, participants include the first 70 who accept the invitation.

Another approach has been implemented at the University of New England (Biddeford, Maine). The deans of each of the university colleges, along with the dean of students and representatives from student organizations sponsor the "Deans' Forum." The forums are held twice a semester with agenda items requested by students prior to the forums. Two-way communication is encouraged through informal discussions between students and administrators. The forums provide a mechanism by which students can supply direct feedback to campus administrators. Although these forums were specifically designed for medical and graduate students, they provide an excellent model for collecting input from all adult learners.

The College of Mount St. Joseph (Cincinnati, Ohio) has a unique approach to conducting a needs assessment or gaining other kinds of learner input. To encourage learner response, they established a "Dog Days" event that involves setting up tables in high traffic areas and selling hot dogs for a quarter to those who complete a survey. Incentives that offer fun or food are often the most effective.

These examples illustrate effective ways that institutions can use information gathering to communicate to adult learners that they matter. Other techniques focus less on gathering information and more on recognizing adult learners. A few examples are cited below.

Iowa State University's Office of Adult Learner and Commuter Student Programs (Ames, Iowa) sponsors a "Nontraditional Student Awareness Week." The primary purpose is to educate the campus community about the needs and concerns of nontraditional students. Activities sponsored throughout the week include an information booth in the Union, a special issue of the campus newsletter, a panel discussion about the experiences of nontraditional students, two workshops for faculty, bulletin board displays in critical campus locations, mass mailings to academic advisors and department heads, displays of photo essays produced by nontraditional students, and a brown-bag lunch social. Although the program is directed to increasing campus awareness, it is at the same time a very comprehensive way to communicate to adult learners that they matter.

The University of Arizona's program, "Eggs a la Campus," (Tucson) takes a different approach to recognizing both adult students and university faculty. Each semester, adult students are given cards to invite faculty members to join them for an informal buffet breakfast. Although no formal program is presented during the breakfast, each table has a placard giving interesting facts about the university as well as statistics that describe the adult student population. These placards become great conversation starters. This event is a good example of how

institutions can initiate informal activities that serve to meet
two of the three goals of advocacy.

On some campuses, the less formal advocacy efforts described earlier in this chapter and the identification of avenues
for the adult learner's voice to be heard will fall short of bringing about the type of institutional changes that ensure equal
treatment for adult learners as members of the academic community. On most campuses, considerable attention must be paid
to modifying specific institutional policies and programs before
equity for adult learners is attained.

INFLUENCING MODIFICATION OF ATTITUDES, POLICIES, AND PROGRAMS

The work of Ackell, Epps, Sharp, and Sparks (1982) provides a useful framework for helping advocates assess their institution's status in terms of meeting the needs of adult learners
and identifying where institutional modifications may be required. Ackell et al. proposed a three-stage developmental process: Institutions begin in a laissez-faire stage in which the system
works neither for or against adult learners, and there is no administrative intervention or effort on their behalf. During the
developmental process, institutions move toward the separatist
stage in which adults are segregated from the major student
body and given separate, specially developed programs that usually have lower institutional priority, status, and support than
those provided to traditional students. The third stage is the equity stage: Adults are treated as equals and have access to the
same quality and quantity of service as the 18- to 22-year-olds.
Ten developmental points essential to moving institutions to the
equity stage are outlined. By using these points, advocates can
frame several questions that need to be asked:

1. Is a statement about the education of and commitment to
   serving adult learners included in the institution's mission
   statement?

2. Do the president and executive staff consistently communicate this commitment to faculty and central administrative units?

3. Does the institution's long-range planning consistently incorporate the needs of adult learners?

4. Does the institutional philosophy communicate the commitment to serving older learners as equally important members of the academic community rather than as commodities to be exploited?

5. Do academic policies outline "real" rather than "conventional" requirements?

6. Does course scheduling extend beyond faculty convenience and preference and consider accessibility to adult learners?

7. Do academic rules and regulations consider the life issues of adult learners?

8. Do university offices and support services have extended office hours that respond to the schedules of older students?

9. Are there methods in place to evaluate how well the institution meets adult learner needs?

10. Are student service units held accountable for providing services that specifically address the unique concerns of adult learners?

Advocates can be instrumental in collecting the information needed to answer these questions and in suggesting modifications to institutional attitudes, policies, and programs if the unique needs of adult learners are to be accommodated. A solid foundation of knowledge ensures that advocacy efforts and suggestions are reasonable, sensible, and needed—characteristics that are consistent with the demands of administrators, governing boards, and state agencies for accountability in both policies and practices. Effective advocates will collect data using a variety of the methods described below.

Focus Groups

Many individuals who work with adults have little confidence in their ability to conduct a formal research project, or they are employed in units that have neither the funds nor the administrative support required by such activities. Focus groups represent a low-cost alternative that can provide very important information. Input from these students can facilitate awareness of organizational dynamics as well as identify program strengths and weaknesses. A by-product of participating in such a group can be adult learner affirmation; participants often feel that their thoughts and experiences do matter. To reinforce this perception, some institutions have invited focus group participants to a luncheon where the activity has been carried on in a relaxed setting. It would be wise to extend this idea by conducting a focus group during the dinner hour so that the insights of evening students could also be included.

These groups are usually conducted with 5 to 10 relatively diverse members of the adult learner population. It is desirable to hold several groups involving different learners. A moderator usually employs four or five guiding questions to lead the discussion. These questions should be open-ended and allow for individual interpretation and response. Examples include the following: "Tell us about what things have made your experience as an adult learner positive or less than desirable." "What campus services or resources have been the most beneficial to you?" "What resources did you need that weren't available?" The information gathered can be extremely useful in identifying programs and practices that require modification.

Focus group findings can also be used to help design a survey for eliciting feedback from a greater number of learners. Individuals who don't have the administrative or financial support should explore collaboration with other units. For example, if there is a graduate degree program in college student personnel, a graduate student looking for a thesis or dissertation topic might be interested in pursuing the project. A cooperative undertaking with the institutional research office constitutes another alternative.

Telephone Interviews

Some institutions may prefer to gather information through telephone interviews. Phone surveys allow the caller to clarify responses and pursue related topics in an open-ended manner. They are also more likely to produce a higher response rate, reduce the number of "don't know" or "no" answers, and provide better opportunities for detailed explanations of issues or concerns. Individuals selected to conduct the interviews should be given instructions on how to ask questions, record responses, and probe for additional information. As in any information-gathering effort, a random selection of individuals chosen for the study is desirable to ensure both diversity and representativeness.

Other advantages of this data collection method include the following: (a) It can be relatively inexpensive to implement, especially if adult learners serve as volunteer assistants. Of course, all volunteers need to be trained. Having callers conduct a mock survey before a real one takes place becomes important. (b) The same survey can easily be replicated each year, providing longitudinal data that are useful in identifying trends. (c) Respondents often feel complimented by the idea that their feedback is valuable, adding to the impression that they are important to the institution.

Telephone surveys can be especially useful in gathering information from two groups whose feedback is seldom considered—those who have dropped out and those who failed to enroll after making initial contacts with the institution. Effective advocacy requires input from those whom the institution has not been able to serve well. These individuals are inclined to discard a mail survey, but often can be convinced to share thoughts and reflections over the phone. The insights and experiences of these individuals often differ markedly from those of enrolled students.

The more sources of information used to collect data, the more comprehensive and accurate the picture of the adult learner's experience will become. The technical excellence of standardized instruments that have been field-tested provides real advantages if financial support for this type of assessment is available.

Institutional Self-Assessment

Self-Assessment Using *Focus on Adults*

An earlier chapter mentioned the self-assessment guide entitled *Focus on Adults* (American Council on Education, 2001). College and university presidents, key administrators, faculty, and staff can use this tool both to evaluate how effectively they serve adult learners and to guide future planning. This publication can be purchased from the American Council on Education's Center for Adult Learning and Educational Credentials.

The guide was based on widely accepted tenets that adult learners have different needs, all students are entitled to equal treatment, and involvement maximizes acceptance of change. The instrument includes 29 assessment inventories organized into 7 major areas: (1) mission and objectives; (2) database; (3) outreach; (4) academic policy; (5) practice and curriculum; (6) supports for learning, faculty and staff development, and rewards; and (7) administrative structure and finance. The "Mattering Scales for Adult Students in Higher Education" (1989) discussed earlier is also included in the guide.

A key feature of this guide is its flexibility. Its creators designed it so that it can be used effectively in a variety of institutional types varying from small, private liberal arts colleges to major land-grant universities. A second important feature is that it can be used to conduct a comprehensive assessment of the entire institution or a focused investigation of selected schools, departments, or other units.

Building on the premise that evaluation often generates demand for institutional change, the *Focus on Adults* guide recommends involving individuals at the institution who are likely to be asked to make changes or likely to be affected by them. By soliciting the assistance of a variety of individuals in various units, an individual can use this instrument to encourage partnerships for change.

Self-Assessment Using CAS Standards

Although *Focus on Adults* is currently the most comprehensive tool available to assist institutions in assessing their responsiveness to adult learners, advocates may also want to refer to the standards for professional practice developed by the Council for the Advancement of Standards (CAS) for Student Services/Developmental Programs. Conducting a CAS self-study provides a helpful alternative to the *Focus on Adults* approach.

The CAS standards (1998) were established by the consensus of a national board of directors representing 35 professional associations. Established in 1979, CAS has developed and adopted 25 sets of functional area standards related predominantly to the student services arena. The standards most useful to advocates are those for commuter programs.

As an example of how these standards might be useful in evaluating an institution's responsiveness to adult learners, consider the first functional area standard, which relates to the institution mission. It reads,

> Commuter student programs and services must consider and respond to
> the diverse needs of commuting students and must help these students
> benefit from the institution's total education process. The goals of a
> commuter student program must be: to provide services and facilities to
> meet physical, personal safety, and educational needs of commuting students based on institutional assessment of their needs; to ensure that the
> institution provides commuter students equal access to services and facilities; to make available opportunities to assist commuting students in
> their individual development; and to act as an advocate for commuter
> students. (Council for the Advancement of Standards for Student Services/Developmental Programs, 1998, p. 21)

The standards' focus on meeting needs beyond those of the residential, full-time student is beneficial to anyone working with adult learners because it calls attention to this student sector and provides a powerful incentive to modify programs and student services.

CAS is currently in the final stages of adapting another set of standards, Educational Services for Distance Learners, which are expected to assist adult learner advocates. One statement included in these proposed standards is that,

> Institutions providing distance education in any form must offer commensurate educational services to assist distance learners to achieve their goals. Such services must be commensurate and comparable to educational services provided to conventional learners, and they must meet standards comparable to those of other institutional offerings. Institutions must recognize, however, that the students who select distance education might have different needs than those enrolled in campus-based instruction.

Many institutions have created distance education courses or programs without giving attention to the implications for student support services. These standards, and the institutional self-study guide that accompanies them, should be extremely useful in alerting institutions to the need for enhancing services.

These brief examples are intended to illustrate some of the ways the standards might prove useful to the adult student advocate. Anticipating institutional need for assistance when assessing status with respect to the minimum criteria, CAS published a set of Self-Assessment Guides (SAGs) in 1998. These provide assistance in developing a process for assessing programs and services.

Seven basic steps are necessary to implement a program self-assessment using the CAS Standards and related SAGs:

1. Establish an assessment team.

2. Carefully examine and discuss the standards.

3. Determine whether any of the guidelines will be used to supplement the standards.

4. Compile and analyze documentary evidence.

5. Judge performance using SAGs assessment criterion measures.

6. Describe discrepancies between assessment findings and program practice.

7. Formulate an action plan.

Advocates are encouraged to examine the CAS standards to determine if their institution would benefit from this self-assessment process.

Institutional Self-Assessment—Standards of Good Practice

Advocates for adult learners in higher education are concerned about achieving and maintaining a high level of quality in programs and services. Because adult learners are more often part-time, off-campus, or distance learners, or all of these, both professional groups and regional accrediting associations have developed standards of good practice to guide programs and institutions serving this population. Professional organizations such as the Adult Higher Education Alliance (AHEA), American Council on Education (ACE), and Council for Adult and Experiential Learning (CAEL) have developed a number of standards to guide various programmatic, delivery system, and related institutional policy and services. These standards recognize the importance of quality learning and quality institutional support grounded in the special contexts, experiences, needs, and conditions of the mature adult student.

Guidelines for self-assessment of institutional effectiveness in adult-oriented programs were collaboratively established by AHEA and ACE (Adult Higher Education Alliance, 2000) These principles suggest that adult degree programs should

- have a mission statement that is consistent with the institutional mission; involve faculty and other institutional representatives who are committed to serving older learners and who have the knowledge needed to effectively serve older learners; establish learning outcomes that extend beyond those framed by the curriculum, to include student goals;
- offer classroom experiences that not only meet academic standards but that are also consistent with the characteristics and contexts of adult learners; use a multitude of methods to assess student learning and choose the appropriate method for the learning experience;
- establish policies, procedures and practices consistent with the circumstances of adult learners and offer student services that are accessible and relevant to these learners; have the needed human, fiscal, and learning resources needed to accomplish their mission; and
- consistently conduct thorough program evaluations.

CAEL and the American Productivity Institute recently completed a benchmarking study of select exemplary adult-oriented institutions. This study also proposed key benchmark principles for serving adult learners in higher education (Flint, 1999). The central premise of the report is that adult-learning-oriented institutions should have a culture in which adult-centered learning and sensitivity to learners' needs, flexibility, and communication drive institutional practice. Their delineated principles for effectiveness suggest the following:

- Outreach. The institution conducts its outreach to adult learners by overcoming barriers in time, place, and tradition in order to create lifelong access to educational opportunities.
- Life and Career Planning. The institution addresses adult learners' life and career goals before or at the onset of enrollment in order to assess and align its capacities to help learners reach their goals.
- Financing.The institution promotes choice by using an array of payment options for adult learners in order to expand equity and financial flexibility.
- Assessment of Learning Outcomes. The institution defines and assesses the knowledge, skills and competencies acquired by adult learners both from the curriculum and from life-and-work experience in order to assign credit and confer degrees with rigor.
- Teaching-Learning Process. The institution's faculty uses multiple methods of instruction (including experiential and problem-based methods) for adult learners in order to connect curricular concepts to useful knowledge and skills.
- Student Support Systems. The institution assists adult learners using comprehensive academic and student support systems in order to enhance students' capacities to become self-directed, lifelong learners.
- Technology. The institution uses information technology to provide relevant and timely information and to enhance the learning experience.
- Strategic Partnerships. The institution engages in strategic relationships, partnerships, and collaborations with employers

and other organizations in order to develop and improve educational opportunities for adult learners.

Regional accrediting bodies have sought guiding principles of good practice for adult degree completion programs and have desired standards for monitoring them as part of the accreditation process. In particular, there has been a concern that adult degree programs share the same level of institutional support and oversight as currently provided to traditional young adult programs. A task force formed by the North Central Association of Colleges and Schools (2000) recently published their recommended principles of good practice designed to assist institutional evaluators. Although designed specifically for evaluating member institutions, readers concerned with standards and guidelines for self-assessment will find value in examining these principles in relation to their institutional efforts. This task force, however, wanted to suggest principles based on their regional context and that had been crafted from their regional institutions. Building upon the findings of a survey conducted with their member institutions, their principles relate to each program's mission, the resources available, educational programs and other services provided, program planning, and integrity. In addition, institutions may wish to consider the additional guidelines on assessing prior learning for credit established by the Middle States Association of Colleges and Schools (1996). These guidelines also reflect the earlier work of CAEL and ACE.

Given the prolific growth of adult learners in higher education, institutions can no longer afford to view this adult learner clientele as peripheral and inconsequential to their mission. These standards and principles of good practice should guide future institutional self-assessments of effectiveness in serving adult learners and in offering specialized adult degree programs or delivery formats.

Using Assessment Findings to Take Action

When advocates have identified areas in need of alteration, they would be wise to consider a variety of issues before taking steps to initiate program changes. The institution's history and development, its values and traditions, represent its roots. Understanding those roots provides a key to predicting areas of resistance to change. Such understandings can also provide insight into where advocates might find support for their efforts.

Developing an effective strategy requires answering several questions: What do individuals and units have to gain or lose should new ideas and recommendations be implemented? What degree of change is required? Do program enhancements involve a large financial commitment, major program alterations, or considerable amounts of time? What type of resistance is likely to be encountered? From what sources? Wise advocates will suggest initiating small-scale changes first. Low cost, minor modifications requiring minimal resources can be accomplished fairly easily. Small changes can build momentum and set the stage for a more ambitious agenda. They can also renew the advocate's energy and motivation to address more complex issues.

Schlossberg et al. (1989) suggest that prior to recommending change, advocates should examine the following:

1. Conceptual issues—Do the ideas make sense in an educational setting?

2. Political issues—Whose interests will be threatened or strengthened? Which institutional values will be reinforced or challenged?

3. Feasibility issues—Are the resources required too far out of line with institutional realities?

Adult learner advocates are seldom in a position to initiate important changes directly. Strategies that induce understanding, recognition, and respect from institution policy-makers become crucially important.

There is little doubt that sensitively conceived programs and services are effective. Research (Polson & Erikson, 1988) has confirmed that institutions with administrators who support services for adult learners are more likely than others to provide student support services with extended hours, to sponsor orientation sessions specifically geared to adult learners, to offer preparatory and refresher courses for adults, and to grant credit for prior learning assessment. These institutions also devote more individual time to adult students.

Political action committees, major corporations, and organizations representing a variety of causes are all aware of the important role played by advocates. The conclusions they have reached are equally valid for each segment of higher education. But they are especially important for the segment that includes adult learners because this segment is relatively new, and thus has been without effective representation.

This chapter has identified the rationale for advocacy, some practices that support effective advocacy, and personnel and procedures that make advocacy work. What remaining task must practitioners accomplish? Adopting some guiding principles for serving adults ensures that the advocacy role becomes more effective and more influential. The report of the Commission on Non-Traditional Study (1973) provides an excellent framework for this task. It has been over 25 years since this commission made its six recommendations for how higher education institutions can adequately serve adult learners. Yet the list has contemporary relevance:

1. The focus must be on the students' needs first, the institution's needs second.

2. Students' needs should take precedence over the institution's convenience.

3. Diversity of opportunity, rather than uniform prescription, must be encouraged.

4. Time, space, and course requirements should be deemphasized in favor of competence and performance.

5. There must be concern for all learners, regardless of age and circumstance.

6. Service must be directed both to the degree seeker and to those who seek enrichment through constant or occasional study.

Not all collegiate settings have adopted and adhered to these recommendations, although some have. For institutions that are not yet serving adult learners in optimal ways, the efforts of adult learner advocates can be an important determinant of the timeliness and effectiveness of reform proposals.

APPENDIX A

Professional Organizations

Readers who work with adult learners may find the following listing of organizations helpful in their search for ways to enhance their professional development. Although not all-inclusive, the authors believe this list to be representative of existing organizations that address, either directly or indirectly, the needs of individuals who work with adults in some capacity. Most publish newsletters or journals, or both, and many sponsor conferences or workshops pertinent to understanding how to better serve the older student population. Recently, many have established listservs that facilitate direct sharing among their membership about innovative programs designed for adult learners. Additionally, these listservs frequently serve as a forum where practitioner concerns and questions can be voiced.

American Association of Adult and Continuing Education

This umbrella association serves the diverse needs of individuals who work with adult learners in a variety of settings from military educators to those responsible for continuing professional education. Its mission is to promote adult learning and development by providing leadership in unifying individual adult education practitioners; fostering the development and sharing of information, theory and research, and best practices; promoting professional identity and growth; and advocating policy initiatives. Web site: http://www.aaace.org/

American Association of Higher Education (AAHE)

This association is devoted to addressing a broad range of issues to create effective change at the campus, local, state, and national levels. Its members envision a higher education enterprise that helps all Americans achieve the deep, lifelong learning they need to grow as individuals, participate in the democratic process, and succeed in a global economy. The organization sponsors a variety of special programs such as the AAHE teaching initiative, the forum on faculty roles and rewards, the assessment forum, and service-learning initiatives. Website: http://www.aahe.org/

American Association of Community Colleges (AACC)

This association is the national voice for two-year associate-degree-granting institutions. It provides a national focus and an agenda that promotes, supports, and advances policy initiatives, advocacy, research, educational services for professional growth and renewal, and networking among its membership Website: http://www.aacc.nche.edu/

American College Personnel Association (ACPA)

This association is geared toward helping student affairs professionals better serve learners. The Commission on Commuter and Adult Learners (XVII) is devoted to individuals working with commuter and adult learners. Innovative programs serving the adult and commuter learner are highlighted through national conference presentations as well as through an extensive awards program. Website: http://www.acpa.nche.edu/

American Council on Education (ACE)

American Council on Education is an institutional membership association that offers a forum to advance the interests and goals of higher and adult education. As part of ACE, the Center for Adult Learning and Educational Credentials provides three main programming units: Corporate Programs, including College Credit Recommendation Services (CREDIT); the Credit by Examination Program and a variety of transcript services; its General Education Development Testing Services; and its Military Programs. ACE has recently updated the *Focus on Adults* publication frequently referenced throughout this book, as well as workshops to help institutions assess how well they are meeting adult learner needs on their campuses. Website: http://www.acenet.edu/

Association for Continuing Higher Education (ACHE)

The Association for Continuing Higher Education is an institution-based organization of colleges, universities, and individuals dedicated to the promotion of lifelong learning and excellence in continuing higher education. It emphasizes the importance of lifelong learning and encourages a commitment to higher education, maintaining a membership of institutions and professionals who administer quality continuing higher education programs, as well as offering a variety of professional development opportunities. Website: http://www.charleston.net/org/ache/

Adult Higher Education Alliance

Known as the Alliance, this organization has a specific focus on alternative undergraduate and graduate degree programs. The "Alliance" members are united by their commitment and advocacy for adult students, adult education professionals, alternative degree programs for adults, and research supporting adult higher education. Website: http://www.ahea.org/resources.htm

Association for Non-Traditional Students in Higher Education (ANTSHE)

Adult learners, academic professionals, institutions, and organizations belong to this international organization committed to encouraging support, education, and advocacy for the adult learning community. A highlight of this recently created organization is the involvement of adult learners in the organizational leadership. Website: http://www.antshe.org/

College Board

The College Board states that it is a national, nonprofit membership association focused upon student entry, assessment, and related instructional activities in higher education. The Office of Adult Learning Services (OALS) was established by the College Board (a) to assist colleges with recruitment, instruction, and assessment of adult students, and (b) to assist adults with decisions about college study. Website: http://www.collegeboard. org/prof/

Council for Adult and Experiential Learning (CAEL)

Focused on expanding lifelong learning opportunities for adult learners, this organization includes members from business and industry, government, and labor, as well as higher education communities. CAEL is known for its leadership in establishing standards for prior learning assessment through portfolio evaluation and educational services for adults through workplace learning programs. Website: http://www.cael.org/index2.html

National Association of Student Personnel Administrators (NASPA)

Serving as a voice for student personnel administration, policy and practice, this organization includes student affairs administrators, faculty, and graduate students, as well as corporate and nonprofit higher education supporters. The adult learner-commuter network specifically addresses needs of professionals working with adult learners. Website: http://www. naspa.org/

National Academic Advising Association (NACADA)

This organization consists of professional advisors and counselors, faculty, administrators, and students working to ensure educational development of students. The Adult Learner Commission has an active and diverse membership consisting not only of academic advisors but also of adult learner program directors and others who work with adults in higher education. NACADA has a video-based advisor training program, which includes a focus on advising adult learners. Website: http://www.nacada.ksu.edu/

National Clearinghouse for Commuter Programs (NCCP)

Housed at the University of Maryland, this clearinghouse publishes a practitioner-based newsletter quarterly and provides members an up-to-date compendium of successful and innovative programs and services from campuses across the nation that includes referrals for further information. Website: http://www.inform.umd.edu/NCCP/

University Continuing Education Association (UCEA)

This institution-based association provides national leadership in university continuing education that supports policies, publications, and conferences that advance workforce and professional development. Member institutions provide pre- or post-baccalaureate-level education, or both, to degree-seeking students, students seeking professional credentials, and those seeking learning for its own sake. Website: http://www.nucea.edu/

APPENDIX B

Working with Adult Learners: An Introductory Workshop

To effectively serve adult students, we recommend that you consider developing an introductory workshop on adult learners for your professional staff and faculty. This proposed workshop will acquaint participants with adult characteristics and needs, as well as provide a forum of discussion for understanding adult student learners. The workshop could be sponsored by numerous campus units and facilitated by someone with extensive knowledge about adult learners. Potential sponsors for the workshop might be the division of student affairs, the academic advising center, the campus adult learner program, or a center for faculty teaching and development. Specific content covered in the workshop could be gathered from information found throughout this book. Ideally, the workshop would be limited to no more than 15 to 20 participants, thus maximizing audience participation. A suggested outline for the workshop's content and time frame follows.

Part 1.   Characteristics of Adult Learners

A.   Small Group Exercise (15–20 minutes)

(Time allocated to this activity will depend on number of workshop attendees).

Participants are asked to spend 5 minutes to list as many one-word descriptors that come to mind when they complete the following statements:

1. Adults who return to college want . . .
2. Adults who return to college are . . .
3. Adults return to college may have . . .
4. Adults who return to college need . . .
5. Adults who return to college may lack . . .

The audience should then be asked to share responses to the above questions. If participants do not know one another, they could also be asked to introduce themselves, including their name and their working roles with campus adult learners. The training facilitator may want to either record the participants' answers on flip charts or ask for a volunteer to assist with this task. If the group is large, it might be useful to have multiple flip charts, each labeled with one of the questions; this would assist in the categorizing and processing of responses. Building upon the audience's responses, the trainer can move into a mini-lecture on characteristics of adult learners.

B.   Mini-Lecture — Characteristics of Adult Learners (20–30 minutes)

Content for the mini-lecture should include many of the characteristics found in Chapter 1 and Chapter 4. Some key points to highlight include the following:

1. Multiple Role Commitments

Adult students are engaged in multiple roles that make an impact upon both the time and the energy they can devote to their role as student. The student role is often secondary to that of being a parent, a full-time employee, a community leader, or all of these. Returning to campus frequently requires a reordering of the adult's life so that the demands of this role may be successfully integrated into an already complex life. It is important that these nonacademic interests and commitments be recognized.

2. Rich Quality and Quantity of Life Experiences

Adults have a greater volume and a different quality of life experiences than the traditional-aged student. This experience base can be an asset and a liability in the classroom. It provides a rich resource for learning and a foundation upon which to build new information. In other instances, these experiences can create barriers to learning. Adults' attitudes, values, and beliefs are established as a result of their experiences. When these experiences are in conflict with what is presented in class, adults may need to be encouraged to remain open and flexible to other views.

3.   Off-Campus Directed

Adult lives revolved around off-campus concerns and demands, rather than having a primary focus on the campus world. First, and most important, adults must build academic schedules revolving around their off-campus commitments (such as work and child-related activities). Their schedules must also take into account their commuting time, as well as the time they have to complete campus-based course requirements (such as those that require the use of the library, a lab, or a computer). Second, adults are frequently less concerned with on-campus activities than the traditional-aged student. Their primary connection to the campus is the classroom. As a result, building a positive learning community in the classroom can become critical to adult learners' persistence.

4.   Differing Adult Developmental Tasks

Unlike traditional-aged students who share common life issues of late adolescence with their peers, adult learners are often confronting a variety of different life transitions and developmental issues. These tasks may have triggered their enrollment. Understanding that these transitions and developmental issues may affect not only what the adult learner is confronting while in the classroom but also what they expect from their college experience can be critical to working effectively with this student population.

5.   Supportive Assistance in Confirming Educational Goals

It is often stated that adults frequently enter college with a predetermined educational goal in mind; in many instances, it is this goal that has initiated their return. This does not imply that adults need less assistance in education and career planning. Helping adults determine whether or not the goal they have set for themselves is an accurate and realistic assessment can be central to their satisfaction with the collegiate experience.

6.   Consumer Orientation

Although some adults rely on employer tuition assistance to help cover the cost of their college course work, many are likely to be paying for their own education. Their decision to spend money on tuition is often at the expense of someone or something else—the new car or the family vacation. Adults view education from a consumer point of view—they want their money's worth. Their initial college or university selection is often based on concerns such as whether or not they can complete the course work at convenient times and locations. Once enrolled, adults set high standards for their performance as well as that of the faculty. They want learning to be applicable to problems they confront on a daily basis. Additionally, they expect high quality classroom experiences that consider the various characteristics previously discussed.

C.   Currently Enrolled Adult Learners

To conclude this section of the workshop, facilitators may want to discuss specific characteristics of adults currently enrolled in their institution. Participants often value relevant information on their institution's adult learner characteristics in comparison to institutional statistics and national findings. Additionally, they need to be aware that adult student characteristics vary not only from institution to institution but from year to year. Workshop sponsors, prior to conducting the workshop, may want to explore collecting data about the institutions' currently enrolled adult learners through some of the methods discussed throughout this text.

An effective alternative way to personalize the workshop would be to include adult learners in the agenda. Asking currently enrolled adult learners to participate in a panel discussion might be a particularly effective way to support the points you have made. It is important that panel participants reflect the diversity of adult students enrolled (such as their academic major, ethnicity, full-time or part-time status, and degree-seeking or non-degree-seeking status). Providing panelists with specific topics for discussion prior to the meeting offers them advanced preparation but will also serve to keep their comments focused. (If this option is pursued, the workshop agenda would need to be adjusted to include a break prior to the panel discussion.)

Break with Refreshments (15–20 minutes)

Part 2.   Implications for Practice

This portion of the workshop will help participants consider the ways in which one's everyday practices may need to be altered if they are to address the needs of adult learners. The exercise below includes questions that can be adapted to audiences who are academic advisors, teaching faculty, and/or student affairs personnel.

A.   Paired Exercise—Part 1 (15 minutes)

The workshop leader will ask attendees to respond to three questions (the questions asked depend on the audience). Participants will be asked to work with the person seated next to them. Each pair will make three lists coinciding with the questions. The exercise could be initiated by saying, "Based on the characteristics of adult learners we have just discussed, we would like you to consider the implications for your role by answering the following three questions."

Academic Advisors

1.   What questions might an adult advisee ask an academic advisor?

2.   What questions should an advisor be prepared to ask the older student?

3.   What campus resources do you think an adult learner could use to enhance the advising process?

Faculty Members

1.   What type of classroom teaching activities might an adult student prefer? (Think about your own learning experiences as an adult—what do you want to have happen when you are a participant.)

2.   What type of activities do you currently use that appear to be effective with all students?

3.   What new formats or resources might you utilize that could enhance an adult learners classroom experience?

Student Affairs Personnel

1.   What type of student services might adult learners seek from an institution?

2.   Do you believe the older student needs are currently being met?

3.   In what ways might the institution adjust so that this student population needs might be better addressed?

Break (15 minutes)

During the break participants will be asked to record their answers on flip charts found around the room, (As indicated below, if the group is small, the facilitator could eliminate this activity.)

B.   Paired Exercise—Part 2 (15–20 minutes depending on number of participants)

In order to encourage a large group exchange of the ideas generated, the paired groups should be encouraged to share their discussions with one another. There are a number of ways this can be accomplished. If the group is small, the facilitator may want to ask each pair to share their answers with the rest of the group. Group size may prohibit this type of interaction; therefore, an alternative would be to place flip charts around the room with the various questions posted. Participants could then be asked to write their key ideas on the flip charts. The facilitator could then discuss the ideas in a mini-lecture that coincides with the questions.

C.   Mini-Lecture—Implications for Practice (20 minutes)

After the paired exercise, a brief lecture building upon the three questions can be used to summarize the importance of considering how the characteristics of adult learners make an impact upon everyday practice. The information and suggested resources found in Chapters 4, 5, and 6 would be useful in developing the content of the mini-lecture.

Conclusion and Evaluation:

In addition to summarizing the major workshop concepts, there are a variety of activities the workshop presenter could use to bring closure to the workshop. A technique the trainer may want to use is to give participants two, 3-inch × 5-inch index cards. Participants are asked to reflect on what they have learned in the workshop and are asked to write the following (on the card that they will take with them):

1.   One thing they have learned
2.   One thing they will do differently in the future
3.   One thing they hope to try soon

On the second card (the card that will be left in a box at the back of the room), they will be asked to respond to the following questions:

1.   One thing they found especially helpful
2.   One thing that could have been done differently to better facilitate their learning
3.   One thing they would have liked to have discussed that wasn't addressed?
4.   Are there future workshop topics related to working with adult learners they would like to see presented?

Postscript

For individuals who are specifically interested in advisor training and who may not want to develop their own advising workshop, they should consider two already existing advisor-training programs. (Note: Although both sources cover a broad review of advising-related issues, each has a separate section devoted to advising adult learners.)

1.   The National Academic Advising Association (www. ksu.edu/nacada) has created a faculty advisor training video and manual. The video contains three types of material: eight

advising scenarios, expert commentary on the scenario, and leading questions relating to each scenario. It is accompanied by a detailed facilitator manual.

2. USA Group Noel-Levitz (www.noellevitz.com) has produced "Academic Advising for Student Success and Retention," a video-based training program featuring four videotapes, one of which focuses specifically on advising special populations. Advising adult learners is included as a feature in this videotape. A training manual (Noel-Levitz, 1997a) and participants' manual (Noel-Levitz, 1997b) accompanies the videotapes.

Although professionally developed training materials offer some benefits, developing institution-specific training ensures that participants are involved in examining advising issues directly applicable to their on-campus adult advisees.

For individuals who are interested in further information on teaching adult learners or in serving adults through student services, a number of institutions have conducted campus visits or have exchanged experts and campus leaders who have past involvement in serving or teaching adult students. In addition, this text offers a wide variety of book resources to supplement professional development needs.

REFERENCES

Ackell, E. F., Epps, R. G., Sharp, N. A., & Sparks, H. L. (1982). Adapting the university to adult students: A developmental perspective. *Continuum, 46*, 30–35.

Adult Higher Education Alliance. (2000). *Principles of good practice for alternative and external degree programs for adults*. (2nd ed.). [On-line]. Available: http://www.ahea.org/pogp.htm.

American Council on Education, Center for Adult Learning and Educational Credentials. (2001). *Focus on adults: A self-study guide for postsecondary educational institutions*. Washington, DC: Author.

Angelo, T. A., & Cross, K. P. (1993). *Classroom assessment techniques: A handbook for college teachers*. (2nd ed.). San Francisco: Jossey-Bass.

Apps, J. (1987). Returning to college study: Barriers for adult learning. In D. Boud, & V. Griffin (Eds), *Appreciating adults learning: From the learner's perspective* (pp. 137–146). London: Kogan.

Ashar, H., & Lane, M. (1993, Fall). Focus groups: An effective tool for continuing higher education. *Journal of Continuing Higher Education, 41*(3), 9–13.

Aslanian, C. B., & Brickell, H. M. (1980). *Americans in transition: Life changes as reasons for adult learning*. New York: College Entrance Examination Board.

Astin, A. W. (1985). *Achieving educational excellence*. San Francisco: Jossey-Bass.

Astin, A. W. (1993). *What matters in college: Four critical years revisited*. San Francisco: Jossey-Bass.

Baxter Magolda, M. B. (1992). *Knowing and reasoning in college: Gender-related patterns in students' intellectual development*. San Francisco : Jossey-Bass.

Beal, P. E., & Noel, L. (1980). *What works in student retention*. Iowa City, IA: American College Testing Program.

Bean, J. P., & Metzner, B. S. (1985). A conceptual model of nontraditional undergraduate student attrition. *Review of Educational Research, 55*(4), 485–540.

Bean J. P., & Metzner, B. S. (1996). A conceptual model of nontraditional undergraduate student attrition. In F. Stage, G. Anaya, J. Bean, D. Hossler, & G. Kuh, (Eds), *College students: The evolving nature of research* (pp. 137–173). ASHE reader series. Needham, MA: Simon & Schuster.

Belenky, M. F., Clinchy, B. M., Goldberger, N. R., & Tarule, J. M. (1986). *Women's ways of knowing : The development of self, voice, and mind*. New York : Basic Books.

Bonham, L. A., & Luckie, J. I. (1993). Taking a break in schooling: Why community college students stop out. *Community College Journal of Research and Practice, 17*(3), 257–270.

Breese, J. R., & O'Toole, R. (1994). Adult women students: Development of a transition status. *Journal of College Student Personnel, 35*(3), 183–189.

Brickell, H. M. (1995). *Adults in the classroom*. New York: College Entrance Examination Board.

Brookfield, S. D. (1987). *Developing critical thinkers: Challenging adults to explore alternative ways of thinking and acting*. San Francisco: Jossey-Bass.

Brookfield, S. D. (1990) *The skillful teacher: On technique, trust and responsiveness in the classroom*. San Francisco: Jossey-Bass.

Brookfield, S. D. (1999). *Discussion as a way of teaching: Tools and techniques for democratic classrooms*. San Francisco: Jossey-Bass.

Bruffee, K. A. (1995). *Collaborative learning: Higher education, interdependence, and the authority of knowledge*. Baltimore: John Hopkins University Press.

Carter, B. L. (1982). *Exit interview summary, fall, 1981*. Indianapolis: Indiana University-Purdue University, Office of Student Services.

Casazza, M. E., & Silverman, S. L. (1996). *Learning assistance and developmental education: A guide for effective practice*. San Francisco: Jossey-Bass.

Chronicle of Higher Education. (1998, May 1). p. A72.

Coll, K. M. (1995). Career, personal and educational problems of community college students: Severity and frequency. *NASPA Journal, 32*(4), 270–278.

College Board Office of Adult Learning Services. (1997). *101 Ways Colleges Serve Adult Students*. New York: College Entrance Examination Board.

Commission on Non-Traditional Study. (1973). *Diversity by design.* San Francisco: Jossey-Bass.

Council for the Advancement of Standards for Student Services/Developmental Programs. (1998). *Commuter student programs and services program standards and guidelines: Self-assessment guide.* Washington, DC: Author.

Cranton, P. (1994). *Understanding and promoting transformative learning.* San Francisco: Jossey-Bass.

Crockett, D. S. (1984). *Advising skills, techniques, and resources.* Iowa City, IA: American College Testing Program.

Cross, K. P. (1981). *Adults as learners.* San Francisco: Jossey-Bass.

Daloz, L. A. (1999). *Mentor: Guiding the journey of adult learners.* San Francisco: Jossey-Bass.

Darkenwald, G. G., & Merriam, S. B. (1982). *Adult education: Foundations of practice.* New York: Harper & Row.

Fishback, S. J. (1997). *The cognitive development of adult undergraduate students.* Unpublished dissertation. Kansas State University.

Flint, T. (1999, Spring). Prior learning assessment: A status report. *Assessment and Accountability Forum, 9*(1), 15–16,19.

Flint, T. A., & Associates. (1999). *Best practices in adult learning: A CAEL/APCQ benchmarking study.* Dubuque, IA: Kendall Hunt.

Gabelnich, F., MacGregor, J., Matthews, R. S., & Smith B. L. (1990). *Learning communities: Creating connections among students, faculty, and disciplines.* New Directions for Teaching and Learning, No. 41. San Francisco: Jossey-Bass.

Galbraith, M. W. (1991). *Facilitating adult learning: A transactional process.* Malabar, FL: Krieger.

Galbraith, M. W. (Ed.) (1998). *Adult learning methods.* (2nd ed.). Malabar, FL: Krieger.

Gilbert, S. (1998). *The campus computing survey.* Washington, DC: American Association for Higher Education.

Graham, S., Donaldson, J., Kasworm, C., & Dirkx, J. (2000, April*).* *The experiences of adult undergraduate students: What shapes their learning.* Presentation at the American Educational Research Association, New Orleans, LA.

Grosset, J. M. (1991). Patterns of integration, commitment, and student characteristics and retention among younger and older students. *Research in Higher Education, 32*(2) 159–178.

Habley, W. R. (2000). Current practices in academic advising. In V. N. Gordon, W. R. Habley, & Associates, *Academic advising: A comprehensive handbook* (pp. 35–43). San Francisco: Jossey-Bass.

Hansen, L. S. (1997). *Integrative life planning: Critical tasks for career development and changing life patterns.* San Francisco: Jossey-Bass.

Hayes, E., & Flannery, D. D. (2000). *Women as learners: The significance of gender in adult learning.* San Francisco: Jossey-Bass.

Hiemstra, R. (1991). *Creating environments for effective adult learning.* New Directions for Adult and Continuing Education, No. 50. San Francisco: Jossey-Bass.

Hiemstra, R., & Sisco, B. (1990). *Individualizing instruction: Making learning personal, empowering, and successful.* San Francisco: Jossey-Bass.

Holland, J. L. (1997). *Making vocational choices: A theory of vocational personalities and work environment.* (3rd ed.). Englewood Cliffs, NJ: Prentice Hall.

Hybertson, D., Hulme, E., Smith, W. A., & Holton, M. A. (1992). Wellness in non-traditional-age students. *Journal of College Student Personnel, 33*(1), 50–55.

Isaacson, L. E., & Brown, D. (2000). *Career information, career counseling, and career development.* (7th ed.). Boston: Allyn-Bacon.

Kasworm C. E. (1997). *Adult meaning making in the classroom.* Paper presented at the American Education Research Association. (ERIC Reproduction Document No. ED 410 778)

Kasworm, C. E. (1990). *Transformative contexts in adult higher education.* Paper presented at the Second International Congress for Research on Activity Theory, Lahti, Finland.

Kasworm, C. E. (1993, April). *Lifelong learning: An alternative model of undergraduate participation.* Presentation to the American Education Research Association, Atlanta, Ga.

Kasworm, C. E. (1995a). *Involvement from an adult undergraduate perspective.* Paper presented at the American Educational Research Association, San Francisco.

Kasworm, C. E. (1995b). *Descriptive database of four-year institutions which report adult programs, policies, and services.* Report submitted to the Association for Continuing Higher Education. Knoxville, TN: College of Education.

Kasworm, C. E., & Blowers, S. (1994). *Adult undergraduate students: Patterns of learning involvement.* (Report to OERI, Department of Education, Washington, DC). Knoxville, TN: College of Education, University of Tennessee. (ERIC Reproduction Document No. Ed 376 321)

Kasworm, C. E., & Pike, G. R. (1994). Adult undergraduate students:

Evaluating the appropriateness of a traditional model of academic performance. *Research in Higher Education, 35*(6), 689–710.

Kiger, D. M., & Johnson, J. A. (1997, Spring). Diffusing the adult student's motivation to disengage from a community college's admission process. *Continuing Higher Education, 61,* 104–113.

King, P. M, & Kitchener, K. S. (1994). *Developing reflective judgment: Understanding and promoting intellectual growth and critical thinking in adolescents and adults.* San Francisco: Jossey-Bass.

Knoell, D. M. (1976). *Through the open door: A study of patterns of enrollment and performance in California's community colleges.* Sacramento: California State Postsecondary Education Commission. (ERIC Document Reproduction Service No. ED 119 752)

Knowles, M. (1980). *The modern practice of adult education.* (2nd rev. ed.). Chicago: Association Press/Follett.

Kolb, D. A. (1984). *Experiential learning: Experience as the source of learning and development.* Englewood Cliffs, NJ: Prentice Hall.

Kowalski, T. J. (1988). *The organization and planning of adult education.* Albany: State University of New York Press.

Kruger, K. (2000). Using information technology to create communities of learners. In Jacoby, B. (Ed.), *Involving commuter students in learning,* New Directions for Higher Education, No. 109 (pp.59–70). San Francisco: Jossey-Bass.

Lamdin, L., & Fugate, M. (1997). *Elderlearning: New frontier in an aging society.* Phoenix, AZ: American Council on Education and the Oryx Press.

Lave, J., & Wenger, E. (1991). *Situated learning: Legitimate peripheral participation.* New York: Cambridge University Press.

Lenning, O. T., & Ebbers, L. H. (1999). *The powerful potential of learning communities: Improving education for the future.* ASHE ERIC Higher Education Reports, No. 26(6). Washington, DC: George Washington University.

Love, P. G., & Love, A. G. (1995). *Enhancing student learning: Intellectual, social and emotional integration.* ASHE-ERIC Higher Education Report, No. 4. Washington, DC: George Washington University.

MacGregor, J., Cooper, J. L., Smith, K. A., & Robinson, P. (2000). *Strategies for energizing large classes: From small groups to learning communities.* New Directions for Teaching and Learning. No. 81. San Francisco: Jossey-Bass.

Maehl, W. (2000). *Lifelong learning at its best: Innovative practices in adult credit programs.* San Francisco: Jossey-Bass.

Malloch, D. C., & Montgomery D. C., (1996, Spring). Variation in characteristics among adult students. *Continuing Higher Education Review,* 60(1), 42–53.

Mangano, J. A., & Corrado, T. J. (1980, August). Re-entry adult students: Needs and implications. *NASPA Forum,1,* 5–7,12.

McClusky, H. Y. (1970). An approach to a differential psychology of the adult potential. In S. M. Grabowski (Ed.), *Adult learning and instruction.* Syracuse, NY: ERIC Clearinghouse on Adult Education.

Merriam, S., & Caffarella, R. (1999). *Learning in adulthood.* (2nd. ed.). San Francisco: Jossey-Bass.

Mezirow, J., & Associates. (1991). *Fostering critical reflections in adulthood: A guide to transformative and emancipatory learning.* Jossey-Bass.

Mezirow, J., & Associates. (1999). *Learning as transformation: Critical perspectives on a theory of practice.* San Francisco: Jossey-Bass.

Middle States Association of Colleges and Schools, Commission on Higher Education. (1996). *Assessing prior learning for credit.* Philadelphia: Author.

Migden, J., & Bradley, L. (1992). Nontraditional alumni survey of satisfaction with the associate's degree. *Community/Junior College Quarterly,* 16(3) 251–259.

Naretto, J. A. (1995). Adult student retention: The influence of internal and external communities. *NASPA Journal, 32* (2), 90–97.

National Center for Education Statistics. (1995). *Profile of older undergraduates: 1989–90.* (Statistical Analysis Report NCES 95–167). Washington, DC: U.S. Department of Education, Office of Educational Research and Improvement.

National Center for Education Statistics. (1996a). *The condition of education.* (Statistical Analysis Report NCES 96–304). Washington, DC: U.S. Department of Education, Office of Educational Research and Improvement.

National Center for Education Statistics. (1996b). *Nontraditional undergraduates: Trends in enrollment from 1986 to 1992 and persistence and attainment among 1989–90 beginning postsecondary students.* (Statistical Analysis Report NCES 97–578). Washington, DC: U.S. Department of Education, Office of Educational Research and Improvement.

National Center for Education Statistics. (1997). *Digest of education statistics 1997.* (Statistical Analysis Report NCES 97–015). Washington, DC: U.S. Department of Education, Office of Educational Research and Improvement.

National Center for Education Statistics. (2000, June). *Postsecondary students with disabilities: Enrollment, services, and persistence. Stats in brief.* (NCES 200–092). Washington, DC: U.S. Department of Education. [On-line: http://nces.ed.gov/pubs2000/2000092.pdf/].

National Clearinghouse for Commuter Programs. (1993). *Serving commuter students: Examples of good practice.* (4th ed.). College Park, MD: Author.

National Clearinghouse for Commuter Programs. (1998). *Serving commuter students: Examples of good practice.* (5th ed.). College Park, MD: Author.

National University Continuing Education Association. (1996). *Lifelong learning trends: A profile of continuing higher education* (4th ed.). Washington DC: Author.

Noel-Levitz. (1997a). *Academic advising for student success and retention: Participants manual.* Iowa City, IA: Author.

Noel-Levitz. (1997b). *Academic advising for student success and retention: Leaders guide.* Iowa City, IA: Author.

North Central Association of Colleges and Schools, Commission on Institutions of Higher Education. (2000). *Task force report on adult degree completion programs and the award of credit for prior learning at the baccaluareate level.* Chicago: Author.

O'Banion, T. (1972). An academic advising model. *Junior College Journal, 42*(6), 62, 64, 66–69.

Palloff, R. M., & Pratt, K. (1999). *Building learning communities in cyberspace: Effective strategies for the on-line classroom.* San Francisco: Jossey-Bass.

Perry, W. B. (1981). Cognitive and ethical growth: The making of meaning. In A. Chickering & Associates (Eds.), *The modern American college* (pp. 76–116). San Francisco: Jossey-Bass.

Polson, C. J. (1993). *Teaching adult students.* (Idea Paper No. 29). Manhattan, KS: Center for Faculty Evaluation and Development.

Polson, C. J. (2000). Using a web page to supplement the advising process. *Mountain Plains Adult Education Association Journal of Adult Education, 28*(1), 44–50.

Polson, C. J., & Eriksen, J. P. (1988). The impact of administrative support and institutional type on adult learner services. *National Academic Advising Journal, 8,* 2, 7–16.

Pratt, D. D. (1998). *Five perspectives on teaching in adult and higher education.* Malabar, Fl: Krieger.

Quinnan, T. (1997). *Adult students "at-risk": Culture bias in higher education.* Westport, CT: Bergin & Garvey.

Robertson, D. L. (1991). Gender differences in the academic progress of adult undergraduates: Patterns and policy implications. *Journal of College Student Development,*32(4), 490–496.

Rosenberg, M., & McCullough, B.C. (1981). Mattering: Inferred significance to parents and mental health among adol scents. In R. Simmons (Ed.), *Research in community and mental 'ealth* (Vol. 2). Greenwich, CT: JAI Press

Santovec, M. L. (1992). *Building diversity: Recruitment a. d retention in the 90s.* Madison, WI: Magna Publications.

Schlossberg, N. K., Lassalle, A.D., & Golec, R. R. (1989). *The mattering scales for adult students in higher education.* Washington DC: Center for Adult Learning, The American Council on Education.

Schlossberg, N. K., Lynch, A. Q., & Chickering, A. W. (Eds.). (1989). *Improving higher education environments for adults: Responsive programs and services from entry to departure.* San Francisco: Jossey-Bass.

Schlossberg, N. K., Waters, E. B., & Goodman, J. (Eds.). (1995). *Counseling adults in transition: Linking practice with theory.* (2nd ed.). New York: Springer.

Sewall, T. (1984). A study of adult undergraduates: What causes them to seek a degree? *Journal of College Student Personnel, 25*(4), 309–314.

Shapiro, N. S., & Levine, J. H. (1999). *Creating learning communities: A practical guide to winning support, organizing for change, and implementing programs.* San Francisco: Jossey-Bass.

Solomon, L. C., & Gordon, J. (1981). *The characteristics and needs of adults in postsecondary education.* Lexington, MA: Lexington Books.

Spanard, J. A. (1990). Beyond intent: Re-entering college to complete the degree. *Review of Educational Research 60,* 309–344

Steltenpohl, E., & Shipton, J. (1986). Facilitating a successful transition to college for adults. *Journal of Higher Education, 44,* 439–452.

Strange, C. C., & Banning, J. H. (2001). *Educating by design: Creating campus learning environments that work.* San Francisco: Jossey-Bass.

Super, D. E. (1990). A life span, life space approach to career development. In D. L. Brown, L. Brooks, and Associates (Eds.), *Career choice and development* (3rd ed.) (pp. 197–261). San Francisco: Jossey-Bass.

Taylor, K., Marienau, C., & Fiddler, M. (2000). *Developing adult learners.* San Francisco: Jossey-Bass.

Tennant, M. C., & Pogson, P. (1995). *Learning and change in the adult years: A developmental perspective.* San Francisco: Jossey-Bass.

Tinto, V. (1987). *Leaving college: Rethinking the causes and cures of student attrition.* Chicago: University of Chicago Press.

Tinto, V. (1997). Classrooms as communities: Exploring the educational characters of student persistence. *Journal of Higher Education, 68*(6), 599–623.

Tisdell, E. J. (1995). *Creating inclusive adult learning environments: Insights from multicultural education and feminist pedagogy.* (Information Series No. 361). Columbus, OH: ERIC Clearinghouse on Adult, Career, and Vocational Education.

University of Tennessee—Knoxville. (2000). Academic policies and regulations, undergraduate retention standards, academic second opportunity. In *Undergraduate catalog 2000-2001* [On-line]. Available: http://pr.utk.edu/undergrad/C__Pol.htm

Vanderpool, N. M., & Brown, W. E. (1994). Implications of a peer telephone network on adult learner GPA and retention. *Journal of College Student Development, 35*(2), 125–128.

Wallace, D. (1979). A comparative analysis of the needs of undergraduate adults. *NASPA Journal, 16*(3), 15–23.

Wenger, E.. (1998). *Communities of practice: Learning, meaning, and identity.* Cambridge, U.K.: Cambridge University Press.

Wlodkowski, R. J. (1999). *Enhancing adult motivation to learn.* San Francisco: Jossey-Bass.

Wlodkowski, R. J., & Ginsberg, M. B. (1995). *Diversity and motivation: Culturally responsive teaching.* San Francisco: Jossey-Bass.

Wright, T., & Spanard, J. (1988, October). *Intent and action: Assessing the gap between adults who would like to re-enter college and those who do.* Paper presented at the American Council of Education/Alliance Meeting, Washington, DC.

INDEX